The Effective Executive in Action

The Effective Executive in Action:
A Journal for Getting the Right Things Done

PETER F. DRUCKER and JOSEPH A. MACIARIELLO

Collins
An Imprint of HarperCollins*Publishers*

Portions of this book are adapted from *"Managing Oneself"* by Peter Drucker *(Harvard Business Review,* January 2005); and *"What Makes an Organization Effective"* by Peter Drucker *(Harvard Business Review,* June 2004)

Also cited are *Good to Great* by Jim Collins (HarperCollins, 2001); *Winning* by Jack Welch (HarperCollins, 2005); *Jack: Straight from the Gut* by Jack Welch (Warner Books, 2001); *Halftime* by Bob Buford (Zondervan, 1994); and *"Peter Drucker on Leadership,"* an interview by Rich Karlgaard *(Forbes.com,* November 19, 2004)

HarperCollins books may be purchased for educational, business, or sales promotional use. For information please write: Special Markets Department, HarperCollins Publishers, 10 East 53rd Street, New York, NY 10022.

Designed by Emily Cavett Taff

Library of Congress Cataloging-in-Publication Data has been applied for.

ISBN-10: 0-06-083262-2
ISBN-13: 978-0-06-083262-9

08   09   10   11   12 DIX/IM 10   9   8   7   6   5   4   3

Effectiveness *can* be learned.
Effectiveness *must* be learned.

—Peter F. Drucker,
The Effective Executive

Contents

Foreword

The key words of this book are *"effective"* and *"action."*

Knowledgeable executives are plentiful; effective executives are much rarer. But executives are not being paid for *knowing*. They are being paid for *getting the right things done*. How to decide what are the right things and how to get them done are the topics of this book—a distillation of sixty years of working with effective executives in business; governments; the military; churches and other non-profits such as universities, museums, hospitals, and trade unions in the United States of America and Canada, the United Kingdom, continental Europe, Japan, and mainland Asia.

This is both a "what to do" and a "how to do it" book. It is also a self-development tool. By using the fill-in sections to record decisions, the reasons underlying them, and the expected results and checking those against actual results, executives and other professional contributors will fast learn what they do well, what they need to improve upon, and what they cannot even do poorly and should not be doing at all. *They will learn where they belong.*

The format of this book was developed by my friend and colleague, Joseph A. Maciariello, who has taught my work for thirty years and knows it much better than I do. Professor Maciariello decided on the topics. He then chose the specific excerpts from my books and works by others, which constitute the text of this work, and wrote the questions. My readers and I are greatly indebted to Professor Maciariello.

However, the book itself should be the comments, actions, decisions, and results recorded by the individual executive using the book as his or her tool to achieve effectiveness.

Peter F. Drucker
Claremont, California
Fall 2005

Introduction

How to Use *The Effective Executive in Action*

The Effective Executive in Action is a companion book to *The Effective Executive.* It provides a step-by-step guide for training yourself to be an effective person, an effective knowledge worker, and an effective executive—for training yourself to get *the right things done.* The book will help you develop habits of effectiveness, to apply wisdom to your tasks.

There are five *practices* or *skills* to acquire to be an effective person. These five are

- Managing your time;
- Focusing your efforts on making contributions;
- Making your strengths productive;
- Concentrating your efforts on those tasks that are most important to results; and
- Making effective decisions.

The first practice, managing your time, and the fourth practice, concentrating your efforts on the most important tasks, are twin pillars upon which effectiveness rests.

You can obtain greater quantities of every other resource except time. Time is your most limiting resource so time management is foundational to getting the right things done. Improving your effectiveness begins by finding out where your time goes and then taking steps to eliminate those tasks that waste your time and the time of others.

Once you have eliminated time wasters the second pillar is to set priorities for the use of your time and to concentrate the application of your time to the highest priority tasks. Here you should give priority to those tasks that make the greatest contribution to your organization. Establishing priorities, and concentrating your efforts on them, is a skill that requires foresight and courage.

The remaining skills rest upon these twin pillars of time management and concentration on priorities.

To get the right things done you must learn to focus your time and effort upon the tasks that will produce results for your organization. Here you are first concerned with "what are results for my position?" And then, "how do I go about gaining commitment from others to help me attain these results?"

Next, you must learn to focus on strengths, yours, your subordinates', and your bosses'. You must take steps to develop your talents and the talents of others. Your staffing and appraisal decisions must be made based upon what a person can do, based upon his or her strengths, not on weaknesses. The one exception to the rule of focusing on strengths in staffing decisions is character and integrity. The presence of integrity accomplishes nothing in itself, but its absence in the leaders of your organization faults everything else because of the poor example it sets for others.

The last practice of effectiveness is decision making. Effective executives make effective decisions. Decision making requires that you take specific steps, such as making sure you have defined the problem correctly and have established correct specifications for an effective decision. But effective decisions often result from a clash of opinions. And decisions are not effective until they are turned into work and are followed up by feedback from their results.

You will not develop into an effective person simply by reading this book. Skills are developed by "doing" and by constant practice.

This book provides you with opportunities to develop your skills. These opportunities consist of questions and actions at the end of each reading. To get the most from this book, you should fill in the open spaces with answers to the questions and action steps that are posed after each reading. The questions and actions are the skill-building exercises in this book.

Questions probe your present practices. They lead you to specific responses. In contrast, actions call for steps to improve your performance and achievement. You should formulate specific actions that are appropriate for managing yourself and organizations.

We suggest that you learn one skill at a time. Each reading in this book is referenced to a section in its source book, *The Effective Executive*. The references at the end of each teaching are to specific and general passages in *The Effective Executive* that pertain to the reading.

The teachings, moreover, have been updated to reflect the numerous writings of Peter Drucker since the publication of *The Effective Executive*. Where Peter Drucker has written or spoken specifically about one of these five practices the material has been incorporated into the primary readings of each chapter.

In addition, the numerous sidebars in this book contain parallel readings from other works of Peter Drucker that refer more generally to each topic. In some of the readings, the sidebars also contain appropriate material from other authors that supplement the point made in the reading.

We wish you success in your pursuit of effectiveness. Remember, with the exception of "integrity," which has to do with "being," the five skills of effectiveness have to do with "doing." Consequently, the skills of effectiveness can only be acquired by practice and more practice.

Effectiveness *can* be learned. Effectiveness *must* be learned.

The Effective Executive in Action

1

Effectiveness Can Be Learned

Introduction

Effectiveness is getting the right things done. It is a *habit* consisting of five complex practices. You can acquire the habit of effectiveness by practice, the way you acquire any other habit.

The practices of the effective executive are five:

- Managing your time;
- Focusing your efforts on making contributions;
- Making your strengths productive;
- Concentrating your efforts on those tasks that are most important to contributions; and
- Making effective decisions.

These practices are simple, deceptively so. But these practices are exceedingly hard to do well. You will have to acquire them, as you learned the multiplication table; that is, repeated *ad nauseam* until "6 x 6 = 36" became an unthinking, conditioned reflex, and a firmly ingrained habit.

Similarly, you learn the five practices of effectiveness by practicing and practicing and practicing them again. (*The Effective Executive*, Chapter 1)

Getting the Right Things Done

To be effective the knowledge worker is, first of all, expected
to get the *right things done*.

*Every knowledge worker in a modern organization is an "executive" if,
by virtue of his or her position or knowledge, he or she is responsible for
a contribution that materially affects the capacity of the organization
to perform and to obtain results.*

The Effective Executive, *pp. 5–9*

Questions

What am I getting paid to do? What should I be paid to do if I
am being paid for *getting the right things done* in my position? Am I
doing things that I shouldn't be doing?

Jack Welch realized that what needed to be done at General Electric when he took over as chief executive was not the overseas expansion he wanted to launch. It was getting rid of businesses that, no matter how profitable, could not be number one or number two in their industries.

Peter F. Drucker, "What Makes an Effective Executive,"
Harvard Business Review, June 2004, p. 59

What Needs to Be Done

Successful leaders don't start out asking, "What do I want to do?" They ask, "What needs to be done?" Then they ask, "Of those things that would make a difference, which are right for me?" They don't tackle things they aren't good at. They make sure other necessities get done, but not by them; they appoint someone else. Successful leaders make sure that they are effective! They are not afraid of strength in others. Andrew Carnegie wanted to put on his gravestone, "Here lies a man who knew how to put into his service men more able than he was himself."

Interview by Rich Karlgaard, "Peter Drucker on Leadership,"
Forbes.com, November 19, 2004

Action

Eliminate or reduce the activities that do not contribute to effectiveness, the things you shouldn't be doing. What are some of these activities?

_____

_____

_____

_____

_____

The Authority of Knowledge

For the authority of knowledge is surely as legitimate as the
authority of position.

*What few yet realize is how many people there are even in the most hum-
drum organization of today, whether business or government agency,
research lab or hospital, who have to make decisions. For the authority
of knowledge is surely as legitimate as the authority of position. These
decisions, moreover, are of the same kind as the decisions of top management.*

The Effective Executive, *pp. 8–9*

Questions

How do my decisions affect the overall performance of the organization? What is limiting my ability to make contributions?

> Decisions are made at every level of the organization. . . . The apparently low-level decisions are extremely important in a knowledge-based organization. Knowledge workers are supposed to know more about their areas of specialization—for example, tax accounting—than anybody else, so their decisions are likely to have an impact throughout the company.
>
> Peter F. Drucker, "What Makes an Effective Executive,"
> *Harvard Business Review*, June 2004, p. 61

Actions

List the steps you can take to remove the impediments that limit your ability to make contributions.

_____

_____

_____

_____

_____

_____

_____

_____

Executive Realities

The fundamental problem is the reality around
the executive.

There are four major realities over which the executive has essentially no control. Every one of these realities exerts pressure toward non-results and nonperformance.

1. *The executive's time tends to belong to everybody else.*
2. *Executives are forced [by the flow of events] to keep on "operating."*
3. *The executive is effective only if and when other people make use of what he contributes.*
4. *Finally, the executive is within an organization. He sees the outside only through thick and distorting lenses, if at all.*

The Effective Executive, *pp. 9–14*

Questions

What major events prevent me from focusing on results? Am I a prisoner of inside events and politics?

_____

_____

_____

_____

_____

_____

_____

Actions

Begin to take steps to change your realities to focus on contribution and results. Do not let the flow of events determine what you do.

_____

_____

_____

_____

_____

_____

_____

_____

_____

The Effective Personality

All effective executives have in common is the ability
to get the right things done.

*The effective executives I have seen differ widely in their temperaments
and their abilities, in what they do and how they do it, in their personalities, their knowledge, their interests—in fact in almost everything
that distinguishes human beings. All they have in common is the ability to get the right things done.*

The Effective Executive, *pp. 20–23*

Questions

Who are three effective knowledge workers in my organization? What are their prominent personality traits? How do these
people use these traits to form habits of effectiveness? What does
this tell me about the relationship between personality traits and
effectiveness?

_____

_____

_____

_____

_____

_____

_____

Effective executives differ widely in their personalities, strengths, weaknesses, values, and beliefs. All they have in common is that they get the right things done. Some are born effective. But the demand is too great to be satisfied by extraordinary talent. Effectiveness is a discipline. And like every discipline, effectiveness *can be* learned and *must* be learned.

Peter F. Drucker, "What Makes an Effective Executive,"
Harvard Business Review, June 2004, p. 63

The Transition from Entrepreneur to Large Company CEO

Again, let's start out discussing what *not* to do. Don't try to be somebody else. By now you have your style. This is how you get things done. Don't take on things you don't believe in and that you yourself are not good at. Learn to say no. Effective leaders match the objective needs of their company with their subjective competencies. As a result, they get an enormous amount of things done fast.

Interview by Rich Karlgaard, "Peter Drucker on Leadership,"
Forbes.com, November 19, 2004

The Danger of Charisma

You know, I was the first one to talk about leadership 50 years ago, but there is too much talk, too much emphasis on it today and not enough on effectiveness. The only thing you can say about a leader is that a leader is somebody who has followers. The most charismatic leaders of the last century were Hitler, Stalin, Mao and Mussolini. They were misleaders! Charismatic leadership by itself certainly is greatly overstated. Look, one of the most effective American presidents of the last 100 years was Harry Truman. He didn't have an ounce of charisma. Truman was as bland as a dead mackerel. Everybody who worked for him worshiped him because he was absolutely trustworthy. If Truman said no, it was no, and if he said yes, it was yes. And he didn't say no to one person and yes to the next one on the same issue. The other effective president of the last 100 years was Ronald Reagan. His great strength was not charisma, as is commonly thought, but that he knew exactly what he could do and what he could not do.

Interview by Rich Karlgaard, "Peter Drucker on Leadership,"
Forbes.com, November 19, 2004

Level 5 Leadership

"One of the most damaging trends in recent history is the tendency (especially by boards of directors) to select dazzling, celebrity leaders and to de-select potential Level 5 leaders."

Jim Collins, Good to Great: Why Some Companies Make the Leap . . . and Others Don't, HarperCollins, 2001, p. 39

Actions

Be yourself. Use your personality traits to form habits of effectiveness. Work on weaknesses that limit your effectiveness.

_____

_____

_____

_____

_____

_____

_____

_____

_____

2

Know Thy Time

Introduction

Time is your limiting resource and it is totally irreplaceable in your life. You cannot expand the amount of time you have available per day, week, or year, as you can expand your other resources such as capital and people in your employ.

Yet, everything you do requires your time. This means that your accomplishments and your effectiveness are set, or limited, by the way you manage your time, your scarcest resource.

Unless you manage your time, you will not be able to manage anything else. The management of your time, therefore, is the foundation for your effectiveness. And the good news is that you can manage your time and improve the management of your time with practice and with constant effort. (*The Effective Executive*, Chapter 2)

Time: The Limiting Factor
to Accomplishment

Effective people know that time is the limiting factor. The output limits of any process are set by the scarcest resource. In the process we call "accomplishment," this is time.

Time is also a unique resource. Of the other major resources, money is actually quite plentiful. People—the third limiting resource—one can hire.

But one cannot rent, hire, buy or otherwise obtain more time. The supply of time is totally inelastic. No matter how high the demand, the supply will not go up. Moreover, time is totally perishable and cannot be stored. Yesterday's time is gone forever and will never come back. Time is, therefore, always in exceedingly short supply.

The Effective Executive, *pp. 25–27*

Question

Do I consciously behave as though time is the limiting factor in my life?

_____

_____

_____

_____

_____

_____

_____

Knowledge is useless to executives until it has been translated into deeds. But before springing into action, the executive needs to plan his course. He needs to think about desired results, probable restraints, future revisions, check-in points, and implications for how he'll spend his time.

The action plan is a statement of intentions rather than a commitment. . . . It should be revised often because every success creates new opportunities. So does every failure. . . . A written plan should anticipate the need for flexibility.

In addition, the action plan needs to create a system for checking the results against expectations. . . .

Finally, the action plan has to become the basis for the executive's time management. Time is the executive's scarcest and most precious resource. And organizations . . . are inherently time wasters. The action plan will prove useless unless it's allowed to determine how the executive spends his or her time.

Peter F. Drucker, "What Makes an Effective Executive," *Harvard Business Review*, June 2004, p. 60

Action

Write down the time *you believe* you allocate to your various tasks and responsibilities in a typical week.

_____

_____

_____

_____

_____

_____

_____

Time Management: The Three Steps

Effective executives start by finding out
where their time actually goes.

Effective executives . . . do not start with their tasks. They start with their time. And they do not start out with planning. They start by finding out where their time actually goes. Then they attempt to manage their time and to cut back unproductive demands on their time. Finally they consolidate their "discretionary" time into the largest possible continuing units. This three-step process:

- *recording time,*
- *managing time, and*
- *consolidating time*

is the foundation of executive effectiveness.

The Effective Executive, *p. 25*

Questions

Do I start my work by planning my tasks? Or do I start by planning my time?

_____

_____

_____

_____

_____

_____

_____

Action

Shift from first planning your tasks to first planning your time.

_____

_____

_____

_____

_____

_____

_____

_____

_____

_____

Recording Time

The first step toward executive effectiveness is therefore to record actual time use.

At a minimum effective executives have the log run on themselves for three to four weeks at a stretch. After each such sample, they rethink and rework their schedule.

The Effective Executive, *pp. 35–37*

Questions

Do I record the way I spend my time? How often do I record time usage? What methods do I use? Am I utilizing today's technology effectively to categorize my activities?

_____

_____

_____

_____

Actions

Create a time log, by activity, to determine where your time goes. You may want to ask an assistant to help you do this. Set a frequency to update your time log (e.g., once a week or once a month).

_____

_____

_____

_____

Eliminate Time-Wasters

First one tries to identify and eliminate the things
that need not be done at all.

*I have yet to see a knowledge worker, regardless of rank or station, who
could not consign something like a quarter of the demands on his time
to the wastepaper basket without anybody's noticing their disappear-
ance.*

The Effective Executive, pp. 40–47

Question

Find these time-wasters, by asking, "of each activity in my time
record what would happen if this were not done at all?"

_____

_____

_____

_____

_____

Action

Prune these activities. Don't worry about pruning too harshly.
If you are too harsh you will hear about it soon.

_____

_____

_____

_____

Delegate Activities

I have never seen a knowledge worker confronted with his time record who did not rapidly acquire the habit of pushing on other people everything that he need not do personally. The first look at the time record makes it abundantly clear that there just is not time enough to do the things the executive himself considers important, himself wants to do, and is himself committed to doing. The only way he can get to the important things is by pushing on others anything that can be done by them.

The Effective Executive, *pp. 37–38*

Questions

Which of the activities on my time log could be done by somebody else just as well, if not better? To whom can I delegate these activities? Can technology help me to save time-tracking progress on delegated activities?

_____

_____

_____

_____

_____

_____

_____

_____

How Capable Leaders Blow It

One of the ablest men I've worked with, and this is a long time back, was Germany's last pre-World War II democratic chancellor, Dr. Heinrich Bruning. He had an incredible ability to see the heart of a problem. But he was very weak on financial matters. He should have delegated but he wasted endless hours on budgets and performed poorly. This was a terrible failing during a Depression and it led to Hitler. Never try to be an expert if you are not.

Build on your strengths and find strong people to do the other necessary tasks.

Interview by Rich Karlgaard, "Peter Drucker on Leadership,"
Forbes.com, November 19, 2004

Actions

Do the most important things. Delegate anything that can be done by someone else. Try to utilize technology periodically to check on progress of delegated activities.

_____

_____

_____

_____

_____

_____

_____

_____

_____

_____

Wasting Time of Other People

What do I do that wastes your time
without contributing to your effectiveness?

The manner in which an executive does productive work may . . . be a major waste of somebody else's time. The senior financial executive of a large organization knew perfectly well that the meetings in his office wasted a lot of time. This man asked all his direct subordinates to every meeting, whatever the topic. As a result the meetings were far too large. And because every participant felt that he or she had to show interest, everybody asked at least one question—most of them irrelevant. As a result the meetings stretched on endlessly. But the senior executive had not known, until he asked, that his subordinates too considered the meetings a waste of their time. Aware of the great importance everyone in the organization placed on status and on being "in the know," he had feared that the uninvited people would feel slighted and left out.

The Effective Executive, *pp. 38–40*

Question

Ask your colleagues, "What do I do that wastes your time without contributing to your effectiveness?"

_____

_____

_____

_____

_____

_____

Action

Eliminate all activities that wastes the time of others.

_____

_____

_____

_____

_____

_____

_____

_____

_____

Prune Activities Resulting from Poor Management

The definition of a "routine" is that it makes unskilled people
without judgment capable of doing what it took
near-genius to do before . . .

◦✗◦

*Identify the time-wasters which follow from lack of system or foresight.
The symptom to look for is the recurrent "crisis," the crisis that comes
back year after year. A crisis that recurs a second time is a crisis that
must not occur again. The annual inventory crisis belongs here.*

*A recurrent crisis should always have been foreseen. It can there-
fore either be prevented or reduced to a routine which clerks can manage. The definition of a "routine" is that it makes unskilled people
without judgment capable of doing what it took near-genius to do before; for a routine puts down in systematic, step-by-step form what a
very able man learned in surmounting yesterday's crisis. The recurrent
crisis is not confined to the lower levels of an organization. It afflicts
everyone.*

The Effective Executive, *pp. 40–42*

Question

What are the recurring crises that cause "drama" in my organization?

_____

_____

_____

_____

Actions

For each recurring crisis write out a procedure that solves the problem and assign the application of the procedure to the appropriate person in the organization. Make sure the rule works permanently by checking it periodically.

_____

_____

_____

_____

_____

_____

_____

_____

_____

Overstaffing

Time-waste often results from overstaffing.

There is a fairly reliable symptom of overstaffing. If the senior people in the group . . . spend more than a small fraction of their time, maybe one tenth, on "problems of human relations," on feuds and frictions, on jurisdictional disputes and questions of co-operation, and so on, then the work force is almost certainly too large. People get into each other's way. People have become an impediment to performance, rather than the means thereto. In a lean organization people have room to move without colliding with one another and can do their work without having to explain it all the time.

The Effective Executive, *pp. 43–44*

Question

Are knowledge workers in my organization absorbed by these "problems of human relations?"

_____

_____

_____

_____

_____

_____

_____

_____

_____

Action

Create a lean organization in which people have room to move without colliding with one another.

_____

_____

_____

_____

_____

_____

_____

_____

_____

Malorganization

Another common time-waster is malorganization.
Its symptom is an excess of meetings.

Meetings are by definition a concession to deficient organizations. For one either meets or one works. One cannot do both at the same time. In an ideally designed structure . . . there would be no meetings.

We meet because people holding different jobs have to cooperate to get a specific task done. We meet because the knowledge and experience needed in a specific situation are not available in one head, but have to be pieced together out of the experience and knowledge of several people.

The Effective Executive, *pp. 44–46*

Questions

Do knowledge people in my organization spend more than a fairly small part of their time in meetings? Are these people able to learn and piece together the knowledge they need to work effectively?

_____

_____

_____

_____

_____

_____

Actions

Consolidate the work of groups whose members meet excessively. Evaluate the purpose of each meeting. Drop those meetings without clear purpose.

_____

_____

_____

_____

_____

_____

_____

_____

_____

Malfunction in Information

ぺん

The last major time-waster is malfunction in information. The administrator of a large hospital was plagued for years by telephone calls from doctors asking him to find a bed for one of their patients who should be hospitalized. The admissions people "knew" that there was no empty bed. Yet the administrator almost invariably found a few. The admissions people simply were not informed immediately when a patient was discharged. The floor nurse knew, of course, and so did the people in the front office who presented the bill to the departing patient. The admissions people, however, got a "bed count" made every morning at 5:00 A.M.—while the great majority of patients were being sent home in mid-morning after the doctors had made the rounds. It did not take genius to put this right; all it needed was an extra . . . copy of the chit that goes from the floor nurse to the front office.

The Effective Executive, *pp. 46–47*

Questions

Do I receive data that are outdated or erroneous? How can these data be provided to me more accurately?

_____

_____

_____

_____

_____

_____

Action

Take steps to make certain the data you receive represents timely and accurate information that allows you to take right action.

_____

_____

_____

_____

_____

_____

_____

_____

_____

_____

Create and Consolidate Blocks of Discretionary Time

How much time is there that is "discretionary," that is, available for the big tasks that will really make a contribution?

The method by which one consolidates one's discretionary time is far less important than the approach.

Most people tackle the job by trying to push the secondary, the less productive matters together, thus clearing, so to speak, a free space between them.

The Effective Executive, *pp. 47–51*

Questions

Do I have a method(s) for creating and consolidating discretionary time? What is it? How much discretionary time per week have I been able to carve out?

_____

_____

_____

_____

_____

_____

_____

_____

_____

Actions

Use the processes of recording time and pruning time-wasters to create significant blocks of discretionary time. Compare *your time spent* with what you *thought you spent your time on*. Make sure you give top priority and your best time to those activities for which you are paid.

_____

_____

_____

_____

_____

_____

_____

_____

_____

Effective Use of Discretionary Time

All effective people work on their time management perpetually. They not only keep a continuing log and analyze it periodically. They set themselves deadlines for the important activities, based on their judgment of their discretionary time.

One highly effective man I know keeps two such lists—one of the urgent and one of the unpleasant things that have to be done—each with a deadline. When he finds his deadlines slipping, he knows his time is again getting away from him.

The Effective Executive, *p. 51*

Question

Do I set priorities for the use of my discretionary blocks of time?

_____

_____

_____

_____

_____

_____

_____

_____

_____

Actions

Set deadlines for your discretionary blocks of time for matters you consider important as well as for matters you consider unpleasant. If you find these deadlines slipping, go back to the three steps of time management and recover the lost blocks of discretionary time.

_____

_____

_____

_____

_____

_____

_____

_____

_____

_____

3

Focus on Contribution

Introduction

To be effective you must focus on contribution and ask yourself, "What can I contribute that will significantly affect the performance and the results of the institution I serve?" And this should be followed by the question, "And what self-development do I need to make this contribution today and in the future?"

A focus on contribution will almost always require you to shift away from your own specialty, skills, and department and to what constitutes performance for your entire organization. This, in turn, requires you to focus on the outside where the results are for your organization.

You should make high demands upon yourself because that is the way you will develop. You will grow according to the demands you make on yourself for achievement. If you demand little of yourself, you will remain stunted. If you demand a good deal of yourself, you will grow to giant stature.

Embrace change! One thing that is certain is that tomorrow's opportunities will not look like today's.

Effective people find themselves asking other people in the organization, their superiors, their subordinates, but above all, their colleagues in other areas: "What contribution from me do you require to make *your* contribution to the organization? When do you need this, how do you need it, and in what form?" These questions underline the reality of a knowledge organization: effective work is actually done in and by teams of people of diverse knowledges and skills. (*The Effective Executive,* Chapter 3)

Focus on Contribution: Results, Values, and Developing People

The effective person focuses on contribution.

The focus on contribution is the key to effectiveness: in one's own work—its content, its level, its standards, and its impacts; in one's relations with others—one's superiors, one's associates, one's subordinates; in one's use of the tools of the executive such as meetings or reports.

The focus on contribution turns the executive's attention away from his own specialty, his own narrow skills, his own department, and toward the performance of the whole. It turns his attention to the outside, the only place where there are results.

"Contribution," may mean different things. For every organization needs performance in three major areas: It needs direct results; building of values and their reaffirmation; and building and developing people for tomorrow.

The Effective Executive, *pp. 52–61*

Questions

Do I spend my time and effort focusing on my own specialty? Or do I seek to contribute to the overall mission of my organization?

_____

_____

_____

_____

_____

Action

Focus your contributions on the overall mission of the organization.

_____

_____

_____

_____

_____

_____

_____

_____

_____

Focus on Results

What can I contribute that will significantly affect the performance and the results of the institution I serve?

*The effective person focuses on contribution. He looks up from his work
and outward toward goals. He asks: "What can I contribute that will
significantly affect the performance and the results of the institution I
serve?" His stress is on responsibility.*

The Effective Executive, *pp. 52–53*

Questions

Am I focused on efforts or results for my position? Is my focus
outward and on the performance of the whole?

What Should I Contribute?

Throughout history, the great majority of people never had to ask the question, What should I contribute? They were told what to contribute, and their tasks were dictated either by the work itself—as it was for the peasant or artisan—or by a master or a mistress—as it was for domestic servants.

. . . [T]here is no return to the old answer of doing what you are told or assigned to do. Knowledge workers in particular have to learn to ask a question that has not been asked before: What *should* my contribution be? To answer it, they must address three distinct elements: What does the situation require? Given my strengths, my way of performing, and my values, how can I make the greatest contribution to what needs to be done? And finally, What results have to be achieved to make a difference?

Peter F. Drucker, "Managing Oneself,"
Harvard Business Review, January 2005, p. 106

Level 5 Leadership

"Level 5 leaders are fanatically driven, infected with an incurable need to produce sustained *results*. They are resolved to do whatever it takes to make the company great, no matter how big or hard the decisions."

Jim Collins, *Good to Great: Why Some Companies Make the Leap . . . and Others Don't*, HarperCollins, 2001, p. 39

The Power of Positive Surprise

"When most people think about developing sensational performance, they imagine beating agreed-upon performance goals. That's all well and good.

But an even more effective way to get promoted is to expand your job's horizons to include bold and unexpected activities. Come up with a new concept or process that doesn't just

Actions

List a number of contributions you could make to your organization. Compare these with the contributions you are currently making.

_____

_____

_____

_____

_____

_____

_____

_____

_____

Contribution of Knowledge Workers

❧

Knowledge workers who do not ask themselves, "What can I contribute?" are not only likely to aim too low, they are likely to aim at the wrong things. Above all, they may define their contribution too narrowly.

The Effective Executive, *pp. 61–63*

Question

How do I define my task?

_____

_____

_____

_____

_____

Action

Take time now to define your task broadly so as to aim high and to aim at doing the right thing.

_____

_____

_____

_____

_____

_____

Three Key Performance Areas

All three have to be built into the contribution of
every executive.

*Every organization needs performance in three major areas: It needs di-
rect results; building of values and their reaffirmation; and building and
developing people for tomorrow. If deprived of performance in any one of
these areas, it will decay and die. All three therefore have to be built into the
contribution of every executive.*

The Effective Executive, *pp. 55–57*

Question

How do I affect each of these three performance areas by my
performance?

Actions

Rank the importance of these three performance areas for your position and identify steps you can take now to improve your contribution to one or more of these three areas. Keep track of your progress.

_____

_____

_____

_____

_____

_____

_____

_____

_____

_____

Direct Results

The direct results of an organization are clearly visible, as a rule. In a business, they are economic results such as sales and profits. In a hospital, they are patient care, and so on.

The Effective Executive, *p. 55–56*

Questions

What are direct results for my position? Are direct results for my position ambiguous? How do I measure or assess direct results?

_____

_____

_____

_____

Actions

Think through the best quantitative measures and qualitative assessments of direct results, even where direct results are ambiguous for your position. Use these measurements to assess your results and to eliminate any confusion about results that now exists.

_____

_____

_____

_____

For What Does the Organization Stand?

Any organization also needs a commitment to values and their constant reaffirmation, as a human body needs vitamins and minerals. There has to be something "this organization stands for," or else it degenerates into disorganization, confusion, and paralysis.

The Effective Executive, *p. 56*

Questions

For what values does my organization stand? Am I satisfied with the way these values are "walked out" amongst employees, customers, suppliers, and the community? Are there any symptoms of confusion and paralysis caused by a lack of commitment to values? Do I uphold my organization's values?

_____

_____

_____

_____

_____

_____

_____

_____

_____

Actions

If your values are healthy ones, take steps to continuously reaffirm them to your employees, customers, and suppliers. Make sure your organization stands for something useful to society.

_____

_____

_____

_____

_____

_____

_____

_____

_____

_____

Executive Succession

An organization that is not capable of perpetuating
itself has failed.

*An organization that is not capable of perpetuating itself has failed.
An organization therefore has to provide today the men and women
who can run it tomorrow. It has to renew its human capital. It should
steadily upgrade its human resources.*

*An organization which just perpetuates today's level of vision, ex-
cellence, and accomplishment has lost the capacity to adapt. And since
the one and only thing certain in human affairs is change, it will not
be capable of survival in a changed tomorrow.*

The Effective Executive, *pp. 56–57*

Question

Does my organization have a systematic process for identifying and developing new human talent to meet the needs of tomorrow?

_____

_____

_____

_____

_____

_____

_____

Level 5 Leadership

"Level 5 leaders set up their successors for even greater success in the next generation, whereas egocentric Level 4 leaders often set up their successors for failure."

Jim Collins, *Good to Great: Why Some Companies Make the Leap . . . and Others Don't*, HarperCollins, 2001, p. 39

Human Resources

"Elevate HR to a position of power and primacy in the organization, and make sure HR people have the special qualities to help managers build leaders and careers. In fact, the best HR types are pastors and parents in the same package."

Jack Welch, *Winning*, HarperBusiness, HarperCollins Publishers, 2005, p. 98

Action

Make or recommend changes to the executive succession process in your organization today to meet the challenges posed by rapid change.

_____

_____

_____

_____

_____

_____

_____

_____

Focus on Contribution and People Development

People adjust to the level of the demands made on them.

Focus on contribution by itself is a powerful force in developing people. People adjust to the level of the demands made on them. One who sets his sights on contribution, raises the sights and standards of everyone with whom he works.

Commitment to contribution is commitment to responsible effectiveness. Without it, a man shortchanges himself, deprives his organization, and cheats the people he works with.

The Effective Executive, *p. 57–58*

Questions

What circumstances have led me to grow the most in my professional life? What roles have my expectations and the expectations of others played in my professional growth? How dedicated am I to making a commitment to my organization that I view as a "stretch"?

_____

_____

_____

_____

_____

_____

_____

Action

Once you have identified your strengths and the strengths of subordinates, insist that you and they meet high expectations by utilizing these strengths to the fullest.

_____

_____

_____

_____

_____

_____

_____

_____

_____

_____

Challenges and Contribution

The failures worked much harder in a good many cases.

⌒✌⌒

The men who succeeded in World War II Washington focused on contri-bution. As a result, they changed both what they did and the relative weight they gave to each of the value dimensions in their work. The failures worked much harder in a good many cases. But they did not challenge themselves, and they failed to see the need for redirecting their efforts.

The Effective Executive, *p. 58*

Questions

Am I focused on the right results, those that will make a dif-ference to the performance of my organization? What can I do that no one else can do which, if done really well, would make a difference to this organization?

_____

_____

_____

_____

Actions

Challenge yourself. Redirect your efforts to enhance your contribution. Work smarter.

_____

_____

_____

_____

Executive Failure

The most common cause of executive failure is inability or unwillingness to change with the demands of a new position. The knowledge worker who keeps on doing what he has done successfully before he moved is almost bound to fail.

The Effective Executive, *p. 58*

Questions

What are results for my position to which my contribution ought to be directed? Has the relative importance between the three dimensions of performance changed recently in my position? Am I trying to replicate in my newest assignment the activities I performed in my old one?

_____

_____

_____

_____

Actions

Assume the patterns of behavior that got you the new responsibilities are wrong for your current responsibilities. Figure out the right things to do in your position and the right way to do them.

_____

_____

_____

_____

Communicating Knowledge

The person of knowledge has always been expected to take responsibility for being understood. It is barbarian arrogance to assume that the layman can or should make the effort to understand him, and that it is enough if the man of knowledge talks to a handful of fellow experts who are his peers.

The Effective Executive, *p. 62*

Questions

Do I maximize the use of my knowledge to make contributions to the organization? When appropriate, do I effectively communicate my knowledge to others?

Actions

Ask other people in the organization, your superiors, your subordinates, and your colleagues in other areas: "What contribution from me do you require to make *your* contribution to the organization? When do you need this, how do you need it, and in what form?" Make your specialized knowledge very accessible to those who depend upon it to do their jobs.

Good Human Relations

The focus on contribution by itself supplies the four basic
requirements of effective human relations.

*Knowledge workers in an organization do not have good human rela-
tions because they have a "talent for people." They have good human
relations because they focus on contribution in their own work and in
their relationships with others.*

*The focus on contribution by itself supplies the four basic require-
ments of effective human relations:*

- *communications;*
- *teamwork;*
- *self-development; and,*
- *development of others.*

The Effective Executive, *pp. 63–69*

Question

What are the contributions for which my organization and my
superior should hold me accountable?

_____

_____

_____

_____

_____

_____

_____

Actions

Work with your superiors, colleagues, and subordinates to develop and to maximize your collective contributions. Create a high-spirit team.

Communications

Communications are practically impossible if they are based on the downward relationships.

The harder the superior tries to say something to his or her subordinate, the more likely it is that the subordinate will mis-hear. He or she will hear what he or she expects to hear rather than what is being said.

The Effective Executive, *p. 65–66*

Questions

Do I demand that my subordinates take responsibility for their contribution in their own work? How do I communicate with my superiors and subordinates? Are they downward or upward and parallel?

Actions

Hold your subordinates accountable for communications. Fully utilize your subordinates' knowledge and abilities. Utilize your responsibility for contribution as the basis for communication.

_____

_____

_____

_____

_____

_____

_____

_____

_____

_____

Teamwork

The focus on contribution leads to communications sideways
and makes teamwork possible.

The question, "Who has to use my output for it to become effective?"
immediately shows up the importance of people who are not in line of
authority, either upward or downward, from and to the individual ex-
ecutive. It underlines what is the reality of a knowledge organization:
The effective work is actually done in and by teams of people of diverse
knowledges and skills.

The Effective Executive, *pp. 66–68*

Questions

Do the knowledge workers in my organization work together
voluntarily according to demands of the task? Or, do we work according to formal reporting relationships?

_____

_____

_____

_____

_____

_____

_____

_____

How Organizations Fall Down

Make sure the people with whom you work understand your priorities. Where organizations fall down is when they have to guess at what the boss is working at, and they invariably guess wrong. So the CEO needs to say, "This is what *I* am focusing on." Then the CEO needs to ask of his associates, "What are *you* focusing on?" Ask your associates, "You put this on top of your priority list—why?" The reason may be the right one, but it may also be that this associate of yours is a salesman who persuades you that his priorities are correct when they are not. So, make sure that you understand your associates' priorities and make sure that after you have that conversation, you sit down and drop them a two-page note—"This is what I think we discussed. This is what I think we decided. This is what I think you committed yourself to within what time frame." Finally, ask them, "What do you expect from me as you seek to achieve your goals?"

Interview by Rich Karlgaard, "Peter Drucker on Leadership," *Forbes.com*, November 19, 2004

Actions

Establish the necessary communications so that you understand your colleagues and know each other's needs, goals, and ways of doing things.

Do not rely *only* on written means of communications for creating effective communications.

_____

_____

_____

_____

_____

Individual Self-Development

❦

Individual self-development in large measure depends on the focus on contributions. The man who asks of himself, "What is the most important contribution I can make to the performance of this organization?" asks in effect, "What self-development do I need? What knowledge and skill do I have to acquire to make the contribution I should be making? What strengths do I have to put to work? What standards do I have to set myself?"

The Effective Executive, *p. 68*

Questions

What self-development knowledge and skill do I need to acquire to make effective contributions to my organization? How can I use this knowledge and skill in my responsibilities?

_____

_____

_____

_____

Actions

Develop a plan to obtain the knowledge and skill you require to make the optimum contribution to your organization. Strive for excellence.

_____

_____

_____

_____

Develop Others

The executive who focuses on contribution also stimulates others to develop themselves, whether they are subordinates, colleagues, or superiors. He sets standards which are not personal but grounded in the requirements of the task. At the same time, they are demands for excellence. For they are demands for high aspiration, for ambitious goals, and for work of great impact.

The Effective Executive, *pp. 68–69*

Questions

Do I demand that my subordinates achieve outstanding results? Do I provide all the necessary tools and opportunities for my people to grow in stature? Do I welcome subordinates who are stronger than I am?

_____

_____

_____

_____

Actions

Develop and implement a plan whereby each of your subordinates is encouraged to develop their full potential.

_____

_____

_____

_____

Make Meetings Productive

The key to running an effective meeting is to decide in advance what kind of meeting it will be.

Different kinds of meetings require different forms of preparation and different results:

> *A meeting to prepare a statement, an announcement, or a press release.*
> One member has to prepare a draft beforehand. At meeting's end, a preappointed member has to take responsibility for disseminating the final test.

> *A meeting to make an announcement—for example, an organizational change.*
> This meeting should be confined to the announcement and a discussion about it.

> *A meeting in which one member reports.*
> Nothing but the report should be discussed.

> *A meeting in which several or all members report.*
> Discussion should be limited to clarification. . . . At this kind of meeting all reports should be limited to a preset time.

> *A meeting whose only function is to allow the participants to be in the executive's presence.*
> Senior executives are effective to the extent to which they can prevent such meetings from encroaching on their workdays.
> Peter F. Drucker, "What Makes an Effective Executive,"
> *Harvard Business Review,* June 2004, pp. 62–63

Question

Do I conduct a meeting according to the kind of meeting it should be?

_____

_____

_____

_____

_____

_____

_____

_____

_____

How to Lead a 21st-Century Organization

Don't travel so much. Organize your travel. It is important that you see people and that you are seen by people maybe once or twice a year. Otherwise, don't travel. Make them come to see you. Use technology—it is cheaper than traveling. . . . The second thing to say is make sure that your subsidiaries and foreign offices take up the responsibility to keep you informed. So, ask them twice a year, "What activities do you need to report to me?" Also ask them, "What about my activity and my plans do you need to know from _me_?"

Interview by Rich Karlgaard, "Peter Drucker on Leadership,"
Forbes.com, November 19, 2004

Actions

Prepare for and conduct meetings according to their kind and their objectives.

_____

_____

_____

_____

_____

_____

_____

_____

_____

Effective Meetings

The effective person always states at the outset of a meeting the specific purpose and contribution it is to achieve. He makes sure that the meeting addresses itself to this purpose. He does not allow a meeting called to inform to degenerate into a "bull session" in which everyone has bright ideas.

The Effective Executive, *p. 69–70*

Questions

What kind of meetings do I conduct most often? How effective are they?

_____

_____

_____

_____

_____

_____

_____

_____

_____

_____

_____

_____

_____

Actions

State the specific purpose and the specific contribution expected from each meeting.

Determine what kind of meeting it should be and then stick to the appropriate format.

Terminate the meeting as soon as its specific purpose has been accomplished.

Don't raise additional matters for discussion. Sum up the meeting and actions to be taken and adjourn.

Follow up to make sure the action agreed upon at a meeting is taken.

4

Making Strength Productive

Introduction

Your task as an executive is to multiply the performance capacity of individuals in your organization. This means you should make staffing decisions based upon what a person can do and then demand that the person do it.

You cannot build on weaknesses—yours, your bosses', or others'. Therefore, make staffing decisions so as to maximize strengths. This does not mean that you should ignore weaknesses. We all have weaknesses. Rather you should place a person in a position where his or her strengths can be fully utilized and where the presence of weaknesses will not harm performance either in that position or in the organization as a whole.

There is one exception to the rule of building on strengths and covering weaknesses. Character and integrity do not accomplish anything by themselves. But their absence faults everything else. Here, therefore, is the one area where weakness is a disqualification by itself rather than a limitation on performance capacity and strength.

Concentrate on raising the performance of one leader rather than in raising the performance of the entire organization. If the performance of your leadership group is high, the average will tend to go up. Therefore, make sure you put in a leadership position the person who has the strength to do an outstanding job. This requires that you focus on the strengths of the person and dismiss his or her weaknesses as irrelevant unless they hamper the full deployment of the person's strength.

Finally, think through your own strengths and those of your bosses. Ask those who know you well to help you identify your strengths. Work out a plan of continuous learning whereby you further develop these strengths. In the same way, do all you can to make the strengths of your bosses productive by reinforcing their strengths and by shielding them from the effects of their weaknesses. (*The Effective Executive*, Chapter 4)

Purpose of the Organization

To make strength productive is the unique purpose
of the organization.

*The effective executive makes strength productive. He knows that one
cannot build on weakness. To achieve results, one has to use all the
available strengths—the strengths of associates, the strength of the superior, and ones' own strengths. These strengths are true opportunities.
To make strength productive is the unique purpose of the organization.*

*The task of an executive is not to change human beings. Rather,
as the Bible tells us in the Parable of the Talents, the task is to multiply performance capacity of the whole by putting to use whatever
strength, whatever health, whatever aspiration there is in individuals.*

The Effective Executive, *pp. 71, 99*

Questions

Am I attempting to understand the strengths of my colleagues, my subordinates, and my boss? What are these
strengths? How can I put these strengths to their highest use in
my organization?

_____

_____

_____

_____

_____

_____

Actions

Raise the performance capacity of the people in your organization by placing them in positions that match their strengths, their energy levels, and their aspirations.

_____

_____

_____

_____

_____

_____

_____

_____

_____

Staff from Strength

The effective executive fills positions and promotes on the basis of what a man can do. He does not make staffing decisions to minimize weaknesses but to maximize strength.

The Effective Executive, *p. 71*

Questions

In filling positions do I seek people who have specific strengths for the assignment? Or do I look for people who are "well-rounded" without glaring weaknesses?

_____

_____

_____

_____

_____

Actions

Concentrate on what potential candidates can do and determine whether these strengths are the right strengths for a particular assignment.

_____

_____

_____

_____

Weaknesses in People

Where there are peaks, there are valleys.

❦

Strong people always have strong weaknesses too. Where there are peaks, there are valleys. And no one is strong in many areas. Measured against the universe of human knowledge, experience, and abilities, even the greatest genius would have to be rated a total failure.

Performance can only be built on strengths. What matters most is the ability to do the assignment.

The Effective Executive, *pp. 71–78*

Questions

Am I a perfectionist? Do I treat weaknesses in a candidate as limitations or as automatic disqualifiers?

_____

_____

_____

_____

_____

_____

_____

_____

_____

_____

At the same time, feedback will also reveal when the problem is a lack of manners. Manners are the lubricating oil of an organization. It is a law of nature that two moving bodies in contact with each other create friction. This is as true for human beings as it is for inanimate objects. Manners—simple things, like saying "please" and "thank you" and knowing a person's name or asking after her family—enable two people to work together whether they like each other or not. Bright people, especially bright young people, often do not understand this. If analysis shows that someone's brilliant work fails again and again as soon as cooperation from others is required, it probably indicates a lack of courtesy—that is, a lack of manners.

Peter F. Drucker, "Managing Oneself,"
Harvard Business Review, January 2005, p. 102

Actions

Look at the best performing person in your organization. What weaknesses are evident in that person? Seek to remedy those weaknesses in yourself and others that are easily remedied, such as bad manners.

_____

_____

_____

_____

_____

_____

_____

Look for Outstanding Strength

❧

Effective executives never ask "How does he get along with me?" Their question is "What does he contribute?" Their question is never "What can a man not do?" Their question is always "What can he do uncommonly well?" In staffing they look for excellence in one major area, and not for performance that gets by all around.

The Effective Executive, *p. 74*

Questions

Do I look for strong performance in relatively few areas that matter to an assignment? Or is my primary question: "How will he or she get along with me?"

_____

_____

_____

_____

Actions

Look for what a person can do uncommonly well. And, ask if that strength matches the strength required in the assignment. Do not look for excellence across the board in a candidate. Focus on the assignment not on the relationship.

_____

_____

_____

_____

Make Each Job Demanding and Big

The second rule for staffing from strength is to make each job demanding and big. It should have challenge to bring out whatever strength a person may have. It should have scope so that any strength that is relevant to the task can produce significant results.

Only if the job is big and demanding to begin with, will it enable a person to rise to the new demands of a changed situation.
The Effective Executive, *pp. 80–83*

Question

Do I place high demands upon people who have demonstrated real strengths for the assignments I have given them?

Actions

Start out with what a person should be able to do well—and then demand that he or she really do the assignment well. Make high demands and push for excellence.

_____

_____

_____

_____

_____

_____

_____

_____

_____

Make Weaknesses Irrelevant

In an organization one can make strength effective
and weakness irrelevant.

*We can so structure an organization that the weaknesses become a per-
sonal blemish. We can so structure as to make the strength relevant.*

*A good tax accountant in private practice might be greatly ham-
pered by his inability to get along with people. But in an organization
such a man can be set up in an office of his own and shielded from direct contact with other people.*

*There are others who get along with people. First-rate tax account-
ants are a good deal rarer.*

The Effective Executive, *pp. 75–76*

Question

How can I make the strength of each person in my organization effective while making his or her weaknesses irrelevant?

_____

_____

_____

_____

_____

_____

_____

_____

Actions

Identify weaknesses of your people and develop an organization structure that maximizes their collective strengths and shields the organization from any serious weaknesses.

_____

_____

_____

_____

_____

_____

_____

_____

_____

Jobs Structured to Fit Personalities

Structuring jobs to fit personality is almost certain to lead to favoritism and conformity. And no organization can afford either. It needs equity and impersonal fairness in its personnel decisions. And it needs diversity. Or else it will lack the ability to change and the ability for dissent which the right decision demands.

The Effective Executive, *pp. 77–78*

Questions

Do I seek human diversity in filling the positions in my organization?

How do I go about it? Is it based upon race, color, creed, or national origin? Or is it based upon the diversity of strengths required to achieve outstanding performance? Is it based on the question, "Is he or she the person most likely to do an outstanding job?"

_____

_____

_____

_____

_____

_____

_____

_____

Action

Structure jobs impersonally without respect to anything but the strengths the individual brings to perform the assignments required by these jobs.

_____

_____

_____

_____

_____

_____

_____

_____

_____

Decision Steps for Effective Staffing Decisions

❧

There are five decision steps for making strength productive through effective staffing decisions.

    1. *Carefully Think Through the Assignment.*
    2. *Look at Several Qualified People.*
    3. *Study Performance Records to Determine What Each Candidate Has Done Well.*
    4. *Discuss Candidates with Those Who Have Worked with Them.*
    5. *Make Sure the Appointee Understands the Assignment.*

The Effective Executive, *pp. 71–92*

Questions

Do I follow a systematic procedure for selecting people for open positions? What is my success rate in staffing decisions?

_____

_____

_____

_____

_____

_____

_____

_____

_____

Actions

Follow steps 1–5 above in making staffing decisions. If you depart from these steps make sure there is a compelling reason to do so.

_____

_____

_____

_____

_____

_____

_____

_____

_____

Think Through the Assignment

Job descriptions may last a long time, but job assignments
change all the time, often unpredictably.

*The job description of a general commanding a division has not
changed since the time of Napoleon. But the assignment may be to
train a division of raw recruits or it may be to command a division in
combat.*

The Effective Executive, *pp. 78–80*

Questions

Do I seek to staff an open position with a person who best fits *the
general job description* for the position? Or do I seek a person who
has demonstrated strength to perform the *specific assignment*?

_____

_____

_____

_____

Action

Think through the primary assignment of the person who is
to occupy a vacant position that you are now seeking to fill.

_____

_____

_____

_____

Consider Several Qualified People

Formal qualifications, such as those listed in a résumé,
in the personnel file, on a job posting, or in a newspaper
ad, are no more than a starting point. Their absence
disqualifies a candidate.

*The most important thing is that the person and the assignment fit
each other. To find the best fit you must consider at least three to five
candidates.*

The Effective Executive, *pp. 78–80*

Question

What role do formal qualifications, such as those listed in a résumé, fit with the job requirements, and strengths of the candidate, play in my people selection process?

_____

_____

_____

_____

Actions

Consider several qualified people for each position and make sure the person selected and the assignment fit each other.

_____

_____

_____

_____

Study the Performance Records of Candidates

The things a person cannot do are of little importance;
instead, you must concentrate on the things they can do
and determine whether they are the right strengths
for this particular assignment.

*Weaknesses are only limitations, and like the absence of formal qual-
ifications they can rule a candidate out. But performance can only be
built on strengths. What matters most is the ability to do the assignment.*

The Effective Executive, *pp. 78–80*

Questions

Do I rule out people based upon their weaknesses? Or do I
rule them out because of the absence of specific strengths required for the position?

_____

_____

_____

_____

_____

_____

_____

_____

_____

Actions

When filling a position concentrate on the things each candidate has done well. Determine whether what a candidate has done well are the right things for the assignment.

_____

_____

_____

_____

_____

_____

_____

_____

Discuss Candidates with Former Colleagues

One person's judgment alone is worthless. By asking for additional opinions you can learn about strengths that impressed others yet were not noticed by you. But you also are likely to discover weaknesses and limitations you haven't noticed. The best information often comes through informal discussions with a candidate's former bosses and colleagues.

The Effective Executive, *pp. 78–80*

Questions

Do I rely on any one person's judgment when evaluating past performance of a candidate? Do I rely on both formal and informal discussion with a candidate's bosses and colleagues? Do I compare my evaluations with others in my organization who have interviewed the candidate?

_____

_____

_____

_____

_____

_____

_____

_____

Actions

Ask for multiple opinions about a candidate so you can learn about strengths that impressed others yet were not noticed by you. You may discover weaknesses and limitations you haven't noticed.

_____

_____

_____

_____

_____

_____

_____

_____

_____

Appointee Should Understand the Assignment

Although this is the last step in making people decisions, it may be the most important. If you fail to accept this responsibility of making sure that the appointee understands his or her new job, do not blame the new person if he or she ultimately fails. Blame yourself, for you have failed to do your duty as a manager.

✑

... The best way to do this is to ask the new person to carefully think over what they have to do to be a success, and then, 90 days into the job, have him or her commit in writing.

The Effective Executive, *pp. 80–83*

Questions

Have I asked the new appointee their understanding of the appointment? Did I get it in writing? Do I blame the new person if he or she ultimately fails? Or do I blame myself for failing to do my duty as a manager?

_____

_____

_____

_____

_____

_____

_____

Action

Accept responsibility for making sure that the appointee understands his or her new job.

_____

_____

_____

_____

_____

_____

_____

_____

_____

_____

Five Ground Rules for Effective Staffing Decisions

❧

There is no such thing as a perfect record in making people decisions. However, executives who take their people decisions seriously and work hard at getting them right can come close to perfection. In addition to the five steps for people decisions, every successful executive follows five ground rules.

1. *The executive must accept responsibility for any placement that fails.*
2. *The executive does have the responsibility to remove people who do not perform.*
3. *Just because a person doesn't perform in the job doesn't mean that that person is a bad worker whom the organization should let go.*
4. *The executive must try to make the right people decisions for every position.*
5. *Newcomers are best put in an established position where the expectations are known and help is available.*

The Effective Executive, *pp. 71–92*

Question

Which of these staffing ground rules do you follow? Which do you ignore?

_____

_____

_____

_____

Actions

Aim for perfection in your staffing recommendations and decisions while recognizing that perfection will elude you. Follow the five ground rules.

Responsibility for Failed Placements

The executive must accept responsibility for any placement that fails. To blame the non-performer is a cop-out. The executive made a mistake in selecting that particular person.

The Effective Executive, *pp. 89–90*

Question

Do I tend to blame a non-performer for my mistake in placement?

_____

_____

_____

_____

_____

_____

_____

_____

_____

_____

_____

_____

_____

Action

Take responsibility for the mistake if you were the one who made the appointment that resulted in failure.

_____

_____

_____

_____

_____

_____

_____

_____

_____

Responsibility for Removing Non-Performers

"The soldier has a right to competent command."

There is an old military saying, "The soldier has a right to competent command." The incompetent or poor performer, when left in his or her job, penalizes all others and demoralizes the entire organization. And it is also no favor to non-performers to be allowed to stay in a job they are not right for. They know that they are not performing.

The Effective Executive, *pp. 89–90*

Questions

Does my enterprise have the habit of leaving a poor performer in his or her job? Do non-performers demoralize those who depend upon their performance?

_____

_____

_____

_____

_____

_____

_____

_____

_____

_____

Actions

Make sure non-performers know that they are not performing. Take steps to remove these non-performers and then help them get placed where their strengths can be made productive.

Help them to do so by providing them with the candid feedback they need to make the next step in their careers.

_____

_____

_____

_____

_____

_____

_____

_____

_____

Right People Decisions for Every Position

❧

Try to make the right people decisions for every position. An organization can only perform to the capacity of its individual workers; thus people decisions must be right. There are dead-end jobs. But there are no unimportant jobs.

The Effective Executive, *pp. 90–91*

Questions

How close is my organization to performing at an optimal level? How much of the deficit is the result of the people decisions of the organization?

_____

_____

_____

_____

_____

Action

Raise the level of performance of your organization by trying to make right people decisions for every position.

_____

_____

_____

_____

A Second Chance

Just because a person doesn't perform in the job he or she was put in doesn't mean that that person is a poor worker whom the organization should let go. It only means that he or she is in the wrong job.

The Effective Executive, pp. 89–90

Questions

Does my organization give people a second chance in another job that better fits their strengths? If so, what is the success rate of these people in a second job?

_____

_____

_____

_____

_____

_____

People who have failed in a new job should be given the choice to go back to a job at their former level and salary. . . . The very existence of the option can have a powerful effect, encouraging people to leave safe, comfortable jobs and take new risky assignments. The organization's performance depends on employees' willingness to take such chances.

A systematic decision review can be a powerful tool for self-development, too. Checking the results of a decision against expectations shows executives what their strengths are, where they need to improve, and where they lack knowledge or information. It shows them their biases.

Peter F. Drucker, "What Makes an Effective Executive,"
Harvard Business Review, June 2004, p. 61

First Who . . . Then What

"When you know you need to make a people change, act. (Corollary: First be sure you don't have someone in the wrong seat.)"

Jim Collins, *Good to Great: Why Some Companies Make the
Leap . . . and Others Don't*, HarperCollins, 2001, p. 63

. . . [F]inding a job after you have been let go

"The goal, if you've been let go, is to stay out of what I have always referred to as the "vortex of defeat," in which you let yourself spiral into inertia and despair.

Jack Welch, *Winning*, HarperBusiness,
HarperCollins Publishers, 2005, p. 273

Actions

Consider a policy of placing non-performers into another position within the organization after a detailed appraisal of their strengths and of the requirements for the second position. Keep careful track of success rates for these second chances.

_____

_____

_____

_____

_____

Place Newcomers in Established Positions

New major assignments should mainly go to people whose
behaviors and habits are well-known and who have
already earned trust and credibility.

*The common practice of hiring somebody from the outside to fill a new
job is much too risky. No wonder it has an extraordinarily high failure
rate of well over 50 percent.*

The Effective Executive, *pp. 80–83*

Question

Do major new assignments in my organization go to people
whose behaviors and habits are well-known and who have already earned trust and credibility?

_____

_____

_____

_____

_____

_____

_____

_____

_____

> Effective executives put their best people on opportunities rather than on problems.
>
> Peter F. Drucker, "What Makes an Effective Executive,"
> *Harvard Business Review*, June 2004, p. 62

First Who . . . Then What

> "Put your best people on your biggest opportunities, not your biggest problems."
>
> Jim Collins, *Good to Great: Why Some Companies Make the Leap . . . and Others Don't*, HarperCollins, 2001, p. 63

Action

Given the extra risks associated with major new assignments, whenever possible, consider making these appointments from the inside.

Appraise Based on Strengths

*Performance appraisal starts out with a statement of the major contri-
butions expected from a person in past and present positions and a
record of performance against these goals.*

Then it asks six questions:

a) *"What has he done well?"*
b) *"What, therefore, is he likely to be able to do well?"*
c) *"What does he have to learn or to acquire to be able to get the
full benefit from his strength?"*
d) *"If I had a son or daughter, would I be willing to have him or
her work under this person?"*
   i) *"If yes, why?"*
   ii) *"If no, why?"*

The Effective Executive, *pp. 85–87*

Questions

Does the performance appraisal process in my organization
start by focusing on strengths? Does it begin with what a person can do? Does it view weaknesses as limitations to the full
use of strengths and achievement, effectiveness, and accomplishment?

_____

_____

_____

_____

_____

Actions

In performance appraisal, emphasize expected performance based upon the person's strengths. Define what a person must learn to fully capitalize upon his or her strengths. Suggest ways to remedy any weaknesses that presently hinder the full development of a person's strengths.

_____

_____

_____

_____

_____

_____

_____

_____

_____

Character and Integrity

Subordinates, especially bright, young, and ambitious ones, tend to mold themselves after a forceful boss. There is, therefore, nothing more corrupting and more destructive in an organization than a forceful but basically corrupt executive. Such a person might well operate effectively on his own; even within an organization, he might be tolerable if denied all power over others. But in a position of power within an organization he destroys. Here, therefore, is the one area in which weakness in itself is of importance and relevance.

The Effective Executive, *pp. 86–87*

Questions

Do top executives in my organization tolerate a lack of character and integrity in a leader?

Do I realize that character and integrity by themselves do not accomplish anything but their absence faults everything else?

_____

_____

_____

_____

_____

_____

_____

_____

Character Development

We have talked a lot about executive development. We have been mostly talking about developing people's strength and giving them experiences. Character is not developed that way. That is developed inside and not outside. I think churches and synagogues and the 12-step recovery programs are the main development agents of character today.

Interview by Rich Karlgaard, "Peter Drucker on Leadership,"
Forbes.com, November 19, 2004

Character Traits

". . . widen your definition of "right people" to focus more on the character attributes of the person and less on specialized knowledge. People can learn skills and acquire knowledge, but they cannot learn the essential character traits that make them right for your organization."

Jim Collins, *Good to Great: Why Some Companies Make the Leap . . . and Others Don't*, HarperCollins, 2001, pp. 216-217

Action

Do not appoint anyone to a leadership position whose character and integrity are corrupting.

_____

_____

_____

_____

_____

_____

How Do I Manage My Boss?

❦

Everybody has a boss—or almost everybody. And most of us have more than one boss. The human resources person who works on a team has at least two—the HR manager who put her on the team and the manager of the team. The division controller in the big company has at least two bosses: the company's chief accounting or chief financial officer and the division manager. And the trend is for knowledge workers to have an increasing number of bosses, an increasing number of people on whose approval and appraisal they depend, and whose support they need. The boss is not only the key person for pay, promotion and placement; he or she is also the key person for the knowledge worker's effectiveness. No matter how good the knowledge worker's work, if the boss does not act on it, nothing will happen, nothing will get done. Here [in the readings that follow] are seven keys to success in managing bosses.

The Effective Executive, *pp. 93–95*

Questions

How important have high-performing bosses been to my own effectiveness and career? Have I ever given thought to what it would take to manage my bosses?

_____

_____

_____

_____

_____

_____

Action

Make it one of your highest priorities to help your bosses become as effective as they can be.

_____

_____

_____

_____

_____

_____

_____

_____

_____

_____

A Boss List

☙

The first thing to do is to make a "boss list." Put down on a piece of paper everyone to whom you are accountable, everyone who can direct you or your people, everyone who appraises you and your work who is expected to have an opinion about you and your performance, everyone on whom you depend to make effective your work and that of your people. And revise that list once a year and always when your job or your assignment changes. It's unlikely to be the same list for longer than a year or so.

The Effective Executive, *pp. 93–95*

Question

Who has the power and is likely to be listened to when he or she has an opinion about me, my performance, my work, my competence, and qualifications?

_____

_____

_____

_____

_____

_____

_____

_____

_____

Action

Draw up a boss list, and remember: it is better to have a few more people on the boss list and then take them off rather than to leave off people who should be on it.

_____

_____

_____

_____

_____

_____

_____

_____

_____

Input from Bosses

Second, ask each one on the list for his or her input and give each your input. Ask each person, "What do I do and what do my people do that helps you do your job? And what do we do that hampers you and makes life more difficult for you?"

The Effective Executive, *pp. 93–95*

Questions

What do I or my people do that helps those on my boss list do their job? What do those on my boss list do that hampers me and makes my job more difficult?

_____

_____

_____

_____

Actions

Review your boss list. Identify what each person does to hamper you in performing your job. Let these "bosses" know what hampers you and what you do or don't do that hampers them.

_____

_____

_____

_____

Help Bosses Perform

The secret is that effective executives make the strengths
of the boss productive.

Third, enable your bosses to perform. The secret is that effective executives make the strengths of the boss productive. Above all, the effective executive tries to make fully productive the strengths of his own superior. He does not worry too much over what the boss cannot do.

The effective executive, therefore, asks: "What can my boss do really well? What has he done really well? What does he need to know to use his strength? What does he need to get from me to perform?"

The Effective Executive, *pp. 93–95*

Questions

Does my boss want monthly presentations concerning the performance, plans, and problems of my department? Or does my boss want me to come in every time there is something to report, some problem to solve, or some results to analyze? Does the boss prefer written or oral reports? Does the boss want information first thing in the morning, at the end of the day, or somewhere in between?

_____

_____

_____

_____

_____

_____

Actions

Do not try to reform your boss. Do not try to reeducate your boss to conform to what books or business schools say bosses should be like. Instead, enable each of your bosses to perform as unique individuals. Accept that it is your responsibility to enable your bosses to perform according to their own unique work styles. How should you proceed?

_____

_____

_____

_____

_____

_____

_____

_____

_____

Build on Bosses' Strengths

A manager's task is to make the strengths of people effective
and their weaknesses irrelevant.

*Fourth, play to the bosses' strengths. A manager's task is to make the
strengths of people effective and their weaknesses irrelevant, and that
applies as much to the manager's bosses as it applies to the manager's
subordinates.*

*The effective executive accepts that the boss is human. Because the
superior is human, he has his strengths; but he also has limitations. To
build on his strengths, that is, to enable him to do what he can do, will
make him effective—and will make the subordinate effective. To try to
build on his weaknesses will be as frustrating and as stultifying as to
try to build on the weaknesses of a subordinate.*

The Effective Executive, *pp. 93–95*

Questions

What are the strengths and weaknesses of my boss? How can I
help my boss become successful? What changes would it take in
my behavior to start focusing on the boss's strengths and to
make his or her weaknesses irrelevant?

_____

_____

_____

_____

_____

_____

The Power of Positive Surprise

Change your job in a way that makes the people around you work better and your boss look smarter. Don't just do the predictable.

Jack Welch, *Winning,* HarperBusiness,
HarperCollins Publishers, 2005, p. 281

Don't make your boss use political capital in order to champion you.

Jack Welch, *Winning,* HarperBusiness,
HarperCollins Publishers, 2005, p. 280

Actions

Ask your boss about his or her work habits. Play to your boss's strengths and protect your boss from his or her weaknesses. Do not underestimate your boss.

_____

_____

_____

_____

_____

_____

_____

_____

_____

_____

Keep Bosses Informed

Fifth, keep your bosses informed. It is, I submit, fairly obvious to anyone who has ever looked that people are either "readers" or "listeners" . . .

People who are both readers and listeners—trial lawyers have to be both, as a rule—are exceptions. It is generally a waste of time to talk to a reader. He only listens after he has read. It is equally a waste of time to submit a voluminous report to a listener. He can only grasp what it is all about through the spoken word.

The Effective Executive, *pp. 93–95*

Questions

Is my boss a reader or a listener?

The one infallible and simple way to find out how my boss wishes to be informed is to ask, "How do you want to be informed?"

_____

_____

_____

_____

_____

_____

_____

_____

_____

_____

_____

Actions

Keep your boss informed according to his work style. Do not try to be a psychologist—ask him or her how they prefer to be kept informed.

_____

_____

_____

_____

_____

_____

_____

_____

_____

No Surprises

It is the subordinate's job to protect his or her boss
from all surprises.

Sixth, protect bosses from surprises. In an organization, there is no such thing as a pleasant surprise. To be exposed to a surprise in the organization one is responsible for is humiliating, and usually public humiliation. Thus it is the subordinate's job to protect his or her boss from all surprises. Otherwise they will not trust a subordinate, and with good reason.

The Effective Executive, *pp. 93–95*

Questions

How does each of my bosses wish to receive warnings of possible surprises? Which ones want a full report even if there is only a slight chance of a surprise?

_____

_____

_____

_____

_____

_____

_____

_____

Actions

Think through carefully how each of your bosses should be informed. Remember: different people must be informed differently.

_____

_____

_____

_____

_____

_____

_____

_____

_____

Common Mistakes in Managing the Boss

A person's boss changes and that person keeps on informing
the new boss the way he or she had informed the last boss.

*A person's boss changes and [it is a common mistake] that [the] person
keeps on informing the new boss the way he or she had informed the last
boss. Invariably that leads to disaster. The new boss concludes either
that the subordinate is trying to keep things from him or her or, more
commonly, the new boss concludes the subordinate is just plain
stupid—which by the way is true. If a boss changes, one changes the
way one communicates and informs. And to say it again, the best way
to do this is to go and ask.*

The Effective Executive, *pp. 93–95*

Questions

Do I try to keep my bosses informed in an identical manner?
Even as my bosses change?

_____

_____

_____

_____

_____

_____

_____

_____

> *Why is my boss acting like a jerk?*
>
> "Generally speaking, bosses are not awful to people whom they like, respect, and need. Think hard about your performance."
>
> Jack Welch, *Winning*, HarperBusiness,
> HarperCollins Publishers, 2005, p. 302

Action

As your bosses change, ask them how you should communicate with them.

_____

_____

_____

_____

_____

_____

_____

_____

_____

_____

Managing Oneself

ℰℱ

The average knowledge worker will outlive the average employing organization. Few businesses, for instance, are successful for more than thirty years. But the working life expectancy of the knowledge worker is more likely to be fifty years. And so, for the first time in history, more and more people are going to outlive their employing organizations. And this means something totally new and unprecedented: knowledge workers now have to take responsibility for managing themselves. No one—or very few super-achievers, a Mozart for instance, an Einstein or an Edison—even dreamed in the past of such autonomy and responsibility.

The Effective Executive, *pp. 95–98*

Question

The knowledge capital I possess makes me a capitalist. Have I accepted responsibility for managing my human capital?

_____

_____

_____

_____

_____

_____

_____

_____

Action

Take responsibility for actively managing your knowledge capital and your career.

_____

_____

_____

_____

_____

_____

_____

_____

Steps for Managing Oneself

Managing Oneself Requires You To:

1. *Identify Your Strengths*
2. *Recognize Your Work Style*
3. *Determine How to Make Your Best Contribution*
4. *Take Responsibility for Work Relationships and*
5. *Develop Opportunities for the Second Half of Your Life.*

The Effective Executive, *pp. 93–95*

Identify Your Strengths

All in all, the effective executive tries to be himself; he does not pretend to be someone else. He looks at his own performance and at his own results and tries to discern a pattern. "What are the things," he asks, "that I seem to be able to do with relative ease, while they come rather hard to other people?"

The Effective Executive, *pp. 96–97*

Questions

What am I good at? How have I determined what I am good at?

_____

_____

_____

_____

_____

_____

_____

_____

_____

_____

_____

_____

What Are My Strengths?

Several implications for action follow from feedback analysis. First and foremost, concentrate on your strengths. Put yourself where strengths can produce results.

Second, work on improving your strengths. Analysis will rapidly show where you need to improve skills or acquire new ones. It will also show the gaps in your knowledge—and those can usually be filled. Mathematicians are born, but everyone can learn trigonometry.

Third, discover where your intellectual arrogance is causing disabling ignorance and overcome it. Far too many people—especially those with great expertise in one area—are contemptuous of knowledge in other areas or believe that being bright is a substitute for knowledge. . . . Go to work on acquiring the skills and knowledge you need to fully realize your strengths.

Peter F. Drucker, "Managing Oneself,"
Harvard Business Review, January 2005, p. 102

What Are My Values?

Do not try to change yourself—you are unlikely to succeed. But work hard to improve the way you perform. And try not to take on work you cannot perform or only will perform poorly.

Peter F. Drucker, "Managing Oneself,"
Harvard Business Review, January 2005, p. 104

Actions

Use *feedback analysis* to determine your strengths. Write down every one of your key decisions and key actions along with the results that you expect them to achieve. Nine to twelve months later, check the actual results against expectations. After a time of following this procedure, you should know your strengths by tracking those decisions and actions where actual results fell in line with or exceeded expectations.

_____

_____

_____

_____

_____

_____

_____

_____

_____

Recognize Your Work Style

It is not very difficult to know how we achieve results. By the time one has reached adulthood, one has a pretty good idea as to whether one works better in the morning or at night. One knows whether one works well as a member of a committee or better alone. Some work best under pressure. Others work better if they have a good deal of time and can finish the job long before the deadline. Some are "readers," others "listeners." All this one knows about oneself.

The Effective Executive, pp. 96–97

Questions

What is my work style? Do I like to work alone or with coworkers? Do I like work to be structured, or do I thrive in a constantly changing work environment? Do I thrive under pressure? How do I learn? Am I a reader or a listener? Or both?

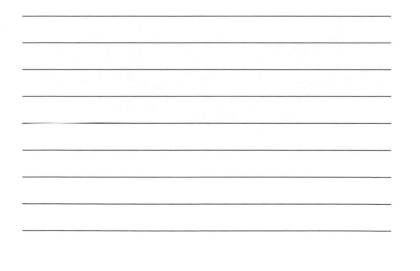

Actions

Figure out your work style. Describe its characteristics and use it to increase your effectiveness. Make sure you fully utilize technology to enhance your work style.

_____

_____

_____

_____

_____

_____

_____

_____

_____

Determine How to Best Make
Your Contribution

One person finds it easy to write up the final report while many others find it a frightening chore. At the same time, however, he or she finds it rather difficult and unrewarding to think through the report and face up to the hard decisions. This person is, in other words, more effective as a staff thinker who organizes and lays out the problems than as the decision maker who takes command responsibility.

✍

The effective executive looks upon people including himself as an opportunity. He knows that only strength produces results.

The Effective Executive, *pp. 95–98*

Question

What assignments will enable me to use my strengths, match my work style, and fit within my value system?

_____

_____

_____

_____

_____

_____

_____

How Do I Perform?

One should waste as little effort as possible on improving areas of low competence. It takes far more energy and work to improve from incompetence to mediocrity than it takes to improve from first-rate performance to excellence. And yet most people—especially . . . teachers and . . . organizations—concentrate on making incompetent performers into mediocre ones. Energy, resources, and time should go instead to making a competent person into a star performer.

Peter F. Drucker, "Managing Oneself,"
Harvard Business Review, January 2005, p. 102

What Are My Values?

To work in an organization whose value system is unacceptable or incompatible with one's own condemns a person both to frustration and to non-performance.

Organizations, like people, have values. To be effective in an organization, a person's values must be compatible with the organization's values. They do not need to be the same, but they must be close enough to coexist. Otherwise, the person will not only be frustrated but also will not produce results.

A person's strengths and the way that person performs rarely conflict; the two are complementary. But there is sometimes a conflict between a person's values and his or her strengths. What one does well—even very well and successfully—may not fit with one's value system. In that case, the work may not appear to be worth devoting one's life to (or even a substantial portion thereof).

Peter F. Drucker, "Managing Oneself,"
Harvard Business Review, January 2005, pp. 104–105

Actions

Think through how you can make the right contribution to your organization. Think through the requirements of your specific situation, your greatest potential contribution and the results that must be achieved. Accept opportunities that suit you and how you work.

_____

_____

_____

_____

_____

_____

_____

_____

Take Responsibility for Work Relationships

Organizations are built on trust, and trust is built on communication and mutual understanding. Thus relationship responsibility is crucial for the modern knowledge worker.

Work relationships depend upon communication. Since communication is a two-way process, you should feel comfortable asking your coworkers to think through and define their own strengths, work styles and values. This is taking responsibility for relationships.

The Effective Executive, *pp. 95–98*

Questions

With whom should I share my work plans, objectives, and goals, and why should I share them with these people? Who depends on me to share this information, and why do they depend on me?

_____

_____

_____

_____

_____

_____

_____

_____

Responsibility for Relationships

Managing yourself requires taking responsibility for relationships. This has two parts. The first is to accept the fact that other people are as much individuals as you yourself are. They perversely insist on behaving like human beings. This means that they too have their strengths; they too have their ways of getting things done; they too have their values. To be effective, therefore, you have to know the strengths, the performance modes, and the values of your coworkers.

The second part of the relationship is taking responsibility for communication. . . . Most of these [conflicts] arise from the fact that people do not know what other people are doing and how they do their work, or what contribution the other people are concentrating on and what results they expect.

Organizations are no longer built on force but on trust. The existence of trust between people does not necessarily mean that they like one another. It means that they understand one another. Taking responsibility for relationships is therefore an absolute necessity. It is a duty.

Peter F. Drucker, "Managing Oneself,"
Harvard Business Review, January 2005, pp. 107–108

Managing Down

Manage your relationships with your subordinates with the same carefulness that you manage the one with your boss.

Jack Welch, *Winning*, HarperBusiness,
HarperCollins Publishers, 2005, p. 288

Think and Say We

Effective executives know that they have ultimate responsibility, which can be neither shared nor delegated. But they have authority only because they have the trust of the organization. This means that they think of the needs and opportunities of the organization before they think of their own needs and opportunities.

Peter F. Drucker, "What Makes an Effective Executive,"
Harvard Business Review, June 2004, p. 63

Actions

Take responsibility for your relationships by:

1. Building on other people's strengths, other people's work styles, and other people's values to attain effective group performance;
2. Letting others know your strengths, work styles, and values, as well as what contribution they should expect from you; and by
3. Providing them information they need in a form they can understand and use.

_____

_____

_____

_____

_____

_____

_____

_____

Develop Opportunities for the Second Half of Your Life

❧

Knowledge workers are able physically to keep on working into old age, and well beyond any traditional retirement age. But they run a new risk: they may become mentally finished. What's commonly called "burnout," the most common affliction of the forty-something knowledge worker, is very rarely the result of stress. Its common, all too common, cause is boredom on the job.

Managing oneself therefore requires that you prepare for the second half of your life.

The Effective Executive, *pp. 95–98*

Questions

Have I begun to prepare myself for the second half of my life? Do I need the challenge of doing something that is new and different? Have I been successful at my work but no longer feel challenged by it? Am I looking for new opportunities for leadership, success, and respect? What can I be doing now to prepare myself for the second half of my life? Do I feel the need to "give back" to society as a result of my own success in life?

The Second Half of Your Life

Knowledge workers outlive organizations, and they are mobile. The need to manage oneself is therefore creating a revolution in human affairs.

Peter F. Drucker, "Managing Oneself,"
Harvard Business Review, January 2005, p. 109

How To Reinvigorate People

Within organizations there are people who, typically in their 40s, hit a midlife crisis when they realize that they won't make it to the top or discover that they are not . . . first-rate. This happens to engineers and accountants and technicians. The worst midlife crisis is that of physicians. . . . They all have a severe midlife crisis. Basically, their work becomes awfully boring. Just imagine seeing nothing for 30 years but people with a skin rash. They have a midlife crisis, and that's when they take to the bottle. How do you save these people? Give them a parallel challenge. Without that, they'll soon take to drinking or to sleeping around. In a coeducational college, they sleep around and drink. The two things are not incompatible, alas! Encourage people facing a midlife crisis to apply their skills in the non-profit sector.

Interview by Rich Karlgaard, "Peter Drucker on Leadership,"
Forbes.com, November 19, 2004

From Success to Significance

"One of the most common characteristics of a person who is nearing the end of the first half is that unquenchable desire to move from success to significance. After a first half of doing what we were supposed to do, we'd like to do something in the second half that is more meaningful—something that rises above the perks and paychecks into the stratosphere of significance."

Bob Buford, *Halftime*, Zondervan Publishing House,
1994, pp. 83–84

> "Significance need not be a 180-degree course change. Instead, do some retrofitting so that you can apply your gifts in ways that allow you to spend more time on things related to what's in your box. And to do it in such a way as to reclaim the thrill of that first deal."
>
> Bob Buford, *Halftime*, Zondervan Publishing House, 1994, p. 89

Actions

Consider a second career that provides some much-needed change. Or, consider a parallel career with a non-profit organization whose values you share.

Consider starting or running a social sector organization that meets a need of society.

List the goals you are striving to achieve in your career, outside of work, or in a possible second career.

_____

_____

_____

_____

_____

_____

_____

_____

_____

_____

5

First Things First

Introduction

The secret of effectiveness lies in concentration of effort. You must make decisions that determine what matters most and, as a result, what comes first. This is how effective executives handle the reality that there is always more to do than time available. But, it is in this way that the executive gets the most done, starting and finishing the most important task before starting the next.

Abandoning what is no longer productive is a major aid to setting priorities and making time to get the highest priority things done. And when you establish priorities you are also forced to establish posteriorities—those tasks that you postpone or perhaps even abandon. Finally, revise your priorities and your posteriorities in light of new realities.

It takes courage to stick to your decisions because what you postpone is often someone else's top priority. If you let pressures make these decisions you are likely to take on tasks that lead you away from major opportunities and away from the work of top management, which is always postponable. (*The Effective Executive*, Chapter 5)

Concentration

Concentration is necessary precisely because the executive
faces so many tasks clamoring to be done.

If there is any "secret" of effectiveness, it is concentration. Effective executives do first things first and they do one thing at a time. There are always more important contributions to be made than there is time available to make them.

The more an executive focuses on upward contribution, the more will the person require fairly big continuous chunks of time. The more he or she switches from being busy to achieving results, the more will the person shift to sustained efforts. Similarly, the more an executive works at making strengths productive, the more will the executive become conscious of the need to concentrate the human strengths available on major opportunities. This is the only way to get results.

This is the "secret" of those people who "do so many things" and apparently so many difficult things. They do only one at a time. As a result, they need much less time in the end than the rest of us. The people who get nothing done often work a great deal harder.

Effective executives do not race. They set an easy pace but keep going steadily. Effective executives know that they have to get many things done. Therefore, they concentrate on doing one thing at a time, and on doing first things first.

Concentration—that is, the courage to impose on time and events his or her own decision as to what really matters and comes first—is the executive's only hope of becoming the master of time and events instead of their whipping boy.

The Effective Executive, *pp. 100–112*

Questions

Do I try to accomplish multiple tasks at one time? Or, do I concentrate on one thing at a time and move deliberately but not frantically through my priorities?

_____

_____

_____

_____

_____

> . . . Welch also thought through another issue before deciding where to concentrate his efforts for the next five years. He asked himself which of the two or three tasks at the top of the list he himself was best suited to undertake. Then he concentrated on that task; the others he delegated. Effective executives try to focus on jobs they'll do especially well. They know that enterprises perform if top management performs—and don't if it doesn't."
>
> Peter F. Drucker, "What Makes an Effective Executive,"
> *Harvard Business Review*, June 2004, p. 59
>
> Napoleon allegedly said that no successful battle ever followed its plan. Yet Napoleon also planned every one of his battles, far more meticulously than any earlier general had done. Without an action plan, the executive becomes a prisoner of events. And without check-ins to re-examine the plan as events unfold, the executive has no way of knowing which events really matter and which are only noise.
>
> Peter F. Drucker, "What Makes an Effective Executive,"
> Harvard Business Review, June 2004, p. 61

Action

Concentrate on doing one thing at a time, and doing the highest priority tasks first.

_____

_____

_____

_____

_____

_____

_____

_____

_____

Abandonment

The first rule for the concentration of executive efforts is to slough off the past that has ceased to be productive.

Organized abandonment requires putting every product, every service, every process, every market or distribution channel and customer, and every end use, on trial for its life on a regular basis.

The Effective Executive, *pp. 104-108*

Question

If I were not making a particular product, performing a specific service, or using a particular process, would I, knowing what I now know, do it now?

_____

_____

_____

_____

_____

Creative Abandonment

A critical question for leaders is, "When do you stop pouring resources into things that have achieved their purpose?" The most dangerous traps for a leader are those near-successes where everybody says that if you just give it another big push it will go over the top. One tries it once. One tries it twice. One tries it a third time. But, by then it should be obvious this will be very hard to do.

Interview by Rich Karlgaard, "Peter Drucker on Leadership," *Forbes.com*, November 19, 2004

A Culture of Discipline

"*Stop* doing" lists are more important than "to do" lists.

Jim Collins, *Good to Great: Why Some Companies Make the Leap . . . and Others Don't*, HarperCollins, 2001, p. 143

No. 1 or No. 2

"The clarity of No. 1 or No. 2 came from a pair of very tough questions Drucker posed: "If you weren't already in the business would you enter it today?" And if the answer is no, "What are you going to do about it?"

Jack Welch, *Straight from the Gut*, Warner Books, Inc., 2001, p. 108

Actions

Commit yourself to the practice of organized abandonment. If the answer to the question above is "no," act to make changes or to abandon the activity.

_____

_____

_____

_____

_____

_____

Where Abandonment Is Always Right

There are at least three cases in which abandonment is always the right decision. The first is the product, service, market, or process that still has some good years of life but is clearly dying. The second is the asset that no longer produces, even though it is fully written off. Finally, the third and most important case is maintaining an old or declining product, service, or market for which the growth of a new product, service, or market is then being stunted.

The Effective Executive, *pp. 104–108*

Questions

Which products, processes, or services in my organization are clearly dying? Which are no longer producing? Which are stunting the growth of a new product or service?

_____

_____

_____

_____

_____

_____

_____

_____

_____

_____

Actions

Abandon products, processes, services, or markets that are no longer serving their intended purpose. Consider establishing a formal abandonment process, such as the one on the next page.

_____

_____

_____

_____

_____

_____

_____

_____

_____

An Abandonment Process

❦

In one fairly big company offering outsourcing services in most developed countries, the first Monday morning of every month is set aside for an abandonment meeting at every management level, from top management to supervisors in each area. Each of these sessions examines one part of the business—one of the services one Monday, one of the regions in which the company does business a month later, the way this or that service is organized the Monday morning of the third month, and so on. Within the year, the company this way examines itself completely, including its people policies, for instance. In the course of a year three to four major decisions are likely to be made on the "what" of the company's services and perhaps twice as many decisions to change the "how." But also each year three to five ideas for new things do come out of these sessions. These decisions to change anything—whether to abandon something, whether to abandon the way something is being done or whether to do something new—are reported each month to all members of management. And twice a year, all management levels report on what has actually happened as a result of these sessions, what action has been taken, and with what results.

Peter F. Drucker, Management Challenges for the 21st Century, *1999, pp. 79–80*

Question

Does my organization abandon things that no longer contribute?

_____

_____

_____

_____

_____

_____

_____

_____

Action

Take the steps necessary to institute or recommend a formal process of abandonment for your organization.

_____

_____

_____

_____

_____

_____

_____

_____

_____

Concentrate on a Few Tasks

Is this still worth doing?

❧

The executive who wants to be effective and who wants his organization to be effective polices all programs, all activities; all tasks. He or she always asks: "Is this still worth doing?" And if it isn't, the executive gets rid of it so as to be able to concentrate on the few tasks that, if done with excellence, will really make a difference in the results of his own job and in the performance of his organization.

The Effective Executive, *p. 106*

Questions

Where is the real value added in my organization? Am I focused on tasks that if done well, will add value and contribute to results?

_____

_____

_____

_____

_____

_____

_____

_____

Your Back Room Is Somebody Else's Front Room

"Peter Drucker gets credit for this one. We practiced it.

Don't run a print shop: Let a printing company do that. It's understanding where your real value added is and putting your best people and resources behind that.

Back rooms by definition will never be able to attract your best."

Jack Welch, *Straight from the Gut,* Warner Books, Inc.,
2001, p. 397

"We took Peter Drucker's advice. We moved the GE 'back rooms' in the United States to the 'front room' in India."

Jack Welch, *Straight from the Gut,* Warner Books, Inc.,
2001, p. 314

Actions

Slough off an old activity before you start on a new one. Stimulate creativity by abandoning the old to create room for the new.

_____

_____

_____

_____

_____

_____

_____

_____

_____

Priorities and Posteriorities

⌇

There are always more productive tasks for tomorrow than there is time to do them and more opportunities than there are capable people to take care of them.

The Effective Executive, *p. 108*

Questions

Do I succumb to the tyranny of the urgent? Do I pay more attention to the flow of events, which clamor for my attention, and in the process sacrifice the truly important tasks?

_____

_____

_____

_____

_____

Check Your Performance

Effective leaders check their performance. They write down, "What do I hope to achieve if I take on this assignment?" They put away their goals for six months and then come back and check their performance against goals. This way, they find out what they do well and what they do poorly. They also find out whether they picked the truly important things to do. I've seen a great many people who are exceedingly good at execution, but exceedingly poor at picking the important things. They are magnificent at getting the unimportant things done. They have an impressive record of achievement on trivial matters.

Interview by Rich Karlgaard, "Peter Drucker on Leadership,"
Forbes.com, November 19, 2004

Prisoner of Your Own Organization

When you are the chief executive, you're the prisoner of your organization. The moment you're in the office, everybody comes to you and wants something, and it is useless to lock the door. They'll break in. So, you have to get outside the office. But still, that isn't traveling. That's being at home or having a secret office elsewhere. When you're alone, in your secret office, ask the question, "What needs to be done?" Develop your priorities and don't have more than two. I don't know anybody who can do three things at the same time and do them well. Do one task at a time or two tasks at a time. That's it. OK, two works better for most. Most people need the change of pace. But, when you are finished with two jobs or reach the point where it's futile, make the list again. Don't go back to priority three. At that point, it's obsolete.

Interview by Rich Karlgaard, "Peter Drucker on Leadership,"
Forbes.com, November 19, 2004

Action

Decide which tasks to give priority and which tasks to postpone.

_____

_____

_____

_____

_____

_____

Postponing the Work of Top Management

Pressures always favor what goes on inside.

Another predictable result of leaving control of priorities to the pressures is that the work of top management does not get done at all. That is always postponable work, for it does not try to solve yesterday's crises but to make a different tomorrow.

Pressures always favor what goes on inside. They always favor what has happened over [as against] the future, the crisis over the opportunity, the immediate and visible over the real, and the urgent over the relevant.

The Effective Executive, *p. 109*

Questions

Do the pressures in my organization always favor yesterday? Does top management pay attention to the outside of the organization or is it consumed by events on the inside?

Actions

Balance the concerns of the present with the opportunities of the future. Keep focused on the issues that are relevant to the job you are supposed to be doing.

_____

_____

_____

_____

_____

_____

_____

_____

_____

Deciding on Posteriorities

The reason why so few executives concentrate is the difficulty of setting "posteriorities"—that is, deciding what tasks not to tackle—and of sticking to the decision.

Most executives have learned that what one postpones, one actually abandons. A good many of them suspect that there is nothing less desirable than to take up later a project one has postponed when it first came up.

The Effective Executive, *p. 110*

Questions

Do I often abandon the tasks I postpone?

Do I try to keep all tasks going—doing a little of each yet not finishing any one? Do I find it difficult to set posteriorities?

_____

_____

_____

_____

_____

_____

_____

_____

_____

_____

Actions

Avoid the tendency of trying to do "just a little bit" of all your tasks. Focus on getting your highest priority tasks done.

_____

_____

_____

_____

_____

_____

_____

_____

_____

_____

Rules for Priority Setting

Aim high, aim for something that will make a difference . . .

Courage rather than analysis dictates the truly important rules for identifying priorities:

- *Pick the future as against the past;*
- *Focus on opportunity rather than on problems;*
- *Choose your own direction—rather than climb on the bandwagon; and*
- *Aim high, aim for something that will make a difference, rather than for something that is "safe" and easy to do.*

The Effective Executive, *p. 111*

Questions

In identifying priorities, do I focus on opportunities or problems? Do I aim high or play it safe?

_____

_____

_____

_____

_____

_____

_____

_____

Actions

Pursue opportunities. Revise your priorities and posteriorities in light of realities. Aim high.

_____

_____

_____

_____

_____

_____

_____

_____

_____

_____

6

Effective Decisions

Introduction

Decision making is the specific activity of the executive. Effective decision making involves a disciplined process and effective decisions have specific characteristics.

The first step in the decision-making process is to determine if a decision is necessary. Once it is determined that a decision is necessary the next step is to classify the decision as either a generic decision to which a generic solution should be sought or a unique decision to which a unique solution should be found. Many problems have been solved before by your organization and the solution should be sought and put into effect.

It is very important to fully understand a problem—to make sure your definition of the problem explains all symptoms that are being observed. Next, you must define the specifications for a solution to the problem. This leads naturally to an answer to the question, "What would be the correct solution to the problem—a solution that meets *all* boundary conditions?"

If a compromise is necessary, you should make sure it goes some way toward solving the problem—that is toward the characteristic of a good compromise. Then you must convert the decision to action and decide who is to take what action and who is accountable for results of the decision. Finally you must follow-up to determine if the decision has produced the desired results.

The right decision requires courage as much as analysis. You should start by soliciting opinions from those knowledgeable about the problem. Test these opinions by asking those who offer their opinions to gather the facts that are necessary to justify their opinion. To make effective decisions, you should develop organized disagreement among those who have different opinions. In this way you will come to better understand the various dimensions of the decision. And once you choose a course of action, by evaluating gains versus risks of each alternative, you will know who is most likely to implement the decision properly. (*The Effective Executive*, Chapters 6 and 7)

Decision Making

To make decisions is the specific executive task.

Good decision makers know that decision making has its own process and its own clearly defined elements and steps. Every decision is risky: it is a commitment of present resources to an uncertain and unknown future. Ignore a single element in the process and the decision will tumble down like a badly built wall in an earthquake. But if the process is faithfully observed and if the necessary steps are taken, the risk will be minimized and the decision will have a good chance of turning out successful.

Decision making is only one of the tasks of an executive. It usually takes but a small fraction of his or her time. But to make decisions is the specific executive task.

The Effective Executive, *pp. 113–114*

Questions

Do I follow a systematic process for making executive decisions? Or do I simply trust my instincts?

_____

_____

_____

_____

_____

_____

Action

Follow the six elements of effective decision-making spelled out in this chapter.

_____

_____

_____

_____

_____

_____

_____

_____

_____

Is a Decision Really Necessary?

Every decision is like surgery. It is an intervention into a system and therefore carries with it the risk of shock. One does not make unnecessary decisions any more than a good surgeon does unnecessary surgery. Individual decision makers, like individual surgeons, differ in their styles. Some are more radical or more conservative than others. But by and large, they agree on the rules, one has to make a decision when a condition is likely to degenerate if nothing is done. This also applies with respect to opportunity. If the opportunity is important and is likely to vanish unless one acts with dispatch, one acts—and one makes a radical change.

The Effective Executive, *p. 155*

Questions

Do I act quickly when a situation I am facing is deteriorating rapidly? Or when an important opportunity is likely to vanish suddenly?

Actions

Do not make unnecessary decisions. But act courageously when a situation is deteriorating rapidly or when a significant opportunity is likely to pass you by if you delay.

_____

_____

_____

_____

_____

_____

_____

_____

_____

Elements of Effective Decision Making

❧

*Executives minimize risk in decision making by following six elements
of effective decision making which are:*

1. *Classifying the Problem*
2. *Defining the Problem*
3. *Specifications of a Decision*
4. *Deciding on What Is Right*
5. *Building Action into the Decision, and*
6. *Testing the Decision Against Actual Results.*

The Effective Executive, *pp. 122–140*

Question

What procedures do I follow in making executive decisions?

_____

_____

_____

_____

_____

_____

_____

_____

_____

Actions

Memorize these six steps and apply them to every complex decision you face.

_____

_____

_____

_____

_____

_____

_____

_____

_____

Classifying the Problem

Is this a generic situation or an exception?

The first question the effective decision-maker asks is: "Is this a generic situation or an exception?" "Is this something that underlies a great many occurrences? Or is the occurrence a unique event that needs to be dealt with as such?" The generic always has to be answered through a rule, a principle. The exceptional can only be handled as such and as it comes. All events but the truly unique require a generic solution. They require a rule, a policy, a principle.

The Effective Executive, *pp. 123–125*

Questions

Is the current decision situation I am facing generic either to my organization or to the industry? Is it a unique event or an early manifestation of a new class of problems? Why am I classifying this decision as either generic or unique?

_____

_____

_____

_____

_____

_____

_____

Actions

Take a recurring crisis that your organization is facing right now. Figure out the cause and establish a generic rule that will resolve all future occurrences of the current crisis.

_____

_____

_____

_____

_____

_____

_____

_____

_____

Defining the Problem

The next key element is defining the problem. This may be the most important element in making effective decisions.

What effective decision makers have learned is to start out with the assumption that the way the problem looks, in all likelihood, is not what it really is. And then they work until they understand the right problem.

Effective decision makers ask:

- *"What is this all about?"*
- *"What is pertinent here?"*
- *"What is key to this situation?"*

The Effective Executive, *pp. 123–130*

Questions

In the past have I picked the wrong answer to the right problem, or, the right answer to the wrong problem? Which of these was easier for me to diagnose and repair?

Actions

Pick a problem you are now facing. Make sure your definition of the problem explains and encompasses all observable facts or symptoms.

Remember: until the definition explains all the observable facts, it is either still incomplete or the wrong definition of the problem. The wrong answer to the right problem will almost always be easier to diagnose and repair than the right answer to the wrong problem.

_____

_____

_____

_____

_____

_____

_____

_____

_____

_____

Specifications of a Decision

The effective person knows that a decision that does not satisfy the boundary conditions is ineffectual and inappropriate.

The third major element in the decision process is clear specifications as to what the decision has to accomplish. What are the minimum goals it has to attain? What is the minimum needed to resolve this problem? The effective executive knows that a decision that does not satisfy the boundary conditions is ineffectual and inappropriate.

The Effective Executive, *pp. 130–134*

Questions

Have I made an incorrect decision recently? What were the boundary conditions the decision should have satisfied? Should I have known in advance that the decision would not achieve its intended purpose?

Actions

Consider a decision you are facing right now. What conditions should the decision satisfy? Articulate these boundary conditions for the decision.

_____

_____

_____

_____

_____

_____

_____

_____

_____

Deciding on What Is Right

❦

One has to start out with what is right rather than what is acceptable (let alone who is right) precisely because one always has to compromise in the end. But if one does not know what is right to satisfy the specifications and boundary conditions, one cannot distinguish between the right compromise and the wrong compromise—and will end up by making the wrong compromise.

The Effective Executive, *pp. 134–136*

Question

What is right for a decision I am now considering?

_____

_____

_____

_____

_____

_____

_____

_____

_____

_____

_____

_____

Asking "What is right for the enterprise?" does not guarantee that the right decision will be made. Even the most brilliant executive is human and prone to mistakes and prejudices. But, failure to ask the question virtually guarantees the wrong decision.

[Executives] know also that a decision that isn't right for the enterprise will ultimately not be right for any of the stakeholders. This . . . practice is especially important for executives at family-run businesses—the majority of businesses in every country—particularly when they are making decisions about people. In the successful family company, a relative is promoted only if he or she is measurably superior to all nonrelatives on the same level.

Peter F. Drucker, "What Makes an Effective Executive,"
Harvard Business Review, June 2004, p. 60 (The order of these two paragraphs is reversed here from their position in the *HBR* article.)

Action

In a situation you are currently facing, start with the steps to achieve the right outcome to the decision you have been considering.

_____

_____

_____

_____

_____

_____

_____

_____

The Right Compromise

"Half a loaf is better than no bread."

There are two different kinds of compromise. One kind is expressed in the old proverb: "Half a loaf is better than no bread." The other kind is expressed in the story of the Judgment of Solomon, which was clearly based on the realization that "half a baby is worse than no baby at all." In the first instance, the boundary conditions are still being satisfied. The purpose of bread is to provide food, and half a loaf is still food. Half a baby, however, does not satisfy the boundary conditions. For half a baby is not half of a living and growing child. It is a corpse in two pieces.

The Effective Executive, *pp. 134–136*

Question

What compromises are acceptable for a decision I am facing right now?

_____

_____

_____

_____

_____

_____

_____

_____

_____

Action

If you must compromise, make the right one; one that at least partially satisfies the boundary conditions.

_____

_____

_____

_____

_____

_____

_____

_____

_____

Building Action into the Decision

Unless a decision has "degenerated into work," it is not a decision; it is at best a good intention.

Converting the decision into action is the fifth major element in the decision process. While thinking through the boundary conditions is the most difficult step in decision-making, converting the decision into effective action is usually the most time-consuming one. Yet a decision will not become effective unless the action commitments have been built into the decision from the start. In fact, no decision has been made unless carrying it out in specific steps has become someone's work assignment and responsibility. Until then, there are only good intentions.

The Effective Executive, *pp. 136–139*

Questions

Have I recently experienced a failure because I didn't convert a right decision into effective action? What steps did I omit?

_____

_____

_____

_____

_____

_____

_____

_____

Actions

Convert a decision you have just made (or are about to make) into action. Specifically, answer these four questions:
1. Who has to know of this decision?
2. What action has to be taken?
3. Who is to take it?
4. What does the action have to be so that the people who have to do it can take it?

_____

_____

_____

_____

_____

_____

_____

_____

_____

Testing the Decision Against Actual Results

Finally, a feedback has to be built into the decision to provide a continual testing, against actual events, of the expectations that underlie the decision. Even the best decision has a high probability of being wrong. Even the most effective one eventually becomes obsolete. One needs organized information for the feedback. One needs reports and figures. But unless one builds one's feedback around direct exposure to reality—unless one disciplines oneself to go out and look—one condemns oneself to a sterile dogmatism and with it ineffectiveness.

The Effective Executive, *pp. 139–142*

Questions

Do I rely exclusively on formal reports on the effects of decisions? Do I go out and obtain firsthand knowledge of results of the decision on a regular basis?

_____

_____

_____

_____

_____

_____

_____

_____

Take Responsibility for Decisions

A decision has not been made until people know:

- the name of the person responsible for carrying it out;
- the deadline;
- the names of the people who will be affected by the decision and therefore have to know about, understand, and approve it—or at least not be strongly opposed to it—and
- the names of the people who have to be informed of the decision, even if they are not directly affected by it.

An extraordinary number of organizational decisions run into trouble because these bases aren't covered. It is just as important to review decisions periodically . . . as it is to make them carefully in the first place. That way, a poor decision can be corrected before it does real damage. These reviews can cover anything from the results to the assumptions underlying the decision.

Peter F. Drucker, "What Makes an Effective Executive,"
Harvard Business Review, June 2004, p. 61

Confront the Brutal Facts

"Conduct autopsies without blame."

Jim Collins, *Good to Great: Why Some Companies Make the Leap . . . and Others Don't,* HarperCollins, 2001, p. 88

Actions

Do not divorce yourself from reality and thereby fall victim to persisting in a course of action long after it has ceased to be appropriate or even rational. Build continuous learning into your work by obtaining feedback from results of the decision. Compare this feedback to the expectations you had when the decision was made.

_____

_____

_____

_____

_____

_____

_____

_____

_____

The Effective Decision

❧

A decision is a judgment. It is a choice between alternatives. It is rarely a choice between right and wrong. It is at best a choice between "almost right" and "probably wrong"—but much more often a choice between two courses of action neither of which is provably more nearly right than the other.

But executives who make effective decisions know that one does not start with facts. One starts with opinions. These are, of course, nothing but untested hypotheses and, as such, worthless unless tested against reality.

The understanding that underlies the right decision grows out of the clash and conflict of divergent opinions and out of the serious consideration of competing alternatives. To get the facts first is impossible. There are no facts unless one has a criterion of relevance. Events by themselves are not facts.

The Effective Executive, *pp. 143–144*

Questions

Do I start my decision-making process by searching for facts? Or do I start with opinions?

_____

_____

_____

_____

_____

_____

_____

Action

Recognize that a decision is a judgment and that there are no facts unless there is a criterion of relevance, that is, a clearly defined problem.

Start with Untested Hypotheses

The only rigorous method . . . that enables us to test an opinion against reality is based on the clear recognition that opinions come first. Then no one can fail to see that we start out with untested hypotheses—in decision-making as in science the only starting point. We know what to do with hypotheses—one does not argue them; one tests them. One finds out which hypotheses are tenable, and therefore worthy of serious consideration, and which are eliminated by the first test against observable experience.

The effective executive encourages opinions. But he insists that the people who voice them also think through what it is that the . . . testing of the opinion against reality—would have to show.

The Effective Executive, *pp. 143–145*

Questions

Do I treat decision making as a process of hypothesis testing as in science? Or do I treat decision making as a search for the "facts" for various alternatives?

_____

_____

_____

_____

_____

_____

_____

_____

Action

Treat the decision-making process as a process of hypothesis testing requiring a criterion of relevance and opinions that must be tested against observable facts.

_____

_____

_____

_____

_____

_____

_____

_____

_____

_____

Opinions Rather Than Facts

The effective executive asks: "What do we have to know
to test the validity of this hypothesis? What would the facts
have to be to make this opinion tenable?"

*And he makes it a habit—in himself and in the people with whom he
works—to think through and spell out what needs to be looked at,
studied, and tested. He insists that people who voice an opinion also
take responsibility for defining what factual findings can be expected
and should be looked for.*

The Effective Executive, *p. 145*

Question

What opinions, with which I start a current decision process,
have to be tested against facts in order for these opinions to form
a tenable hypothesis?

_____

_____

_____

_____

_____

_____

_____

_____

_____

Actions

Think about this decision that you are facing. Seek opinions about the decision from people knowledgeable in the area of the decision. What facts are necessary to support the opinions offered? Ask those who support these opinions to test them against the facts or test them yourself against the facts.

_____

_____

_____

_____

_____

_____

_____

_____

_____

Develop Disagreement

Decisions of the kind the executive has to make are not made well by acclamation.

Unless one has considered alternatives, one has a closed mind. This, above all, explains why effective decision-makers deliberately . . . create dissension and disagreement, rather than consensus. Decisions of the kind the executive has to make are not made well by acclamation. They are made well only if based on the clash of conflicting views, the dialogue between different points of view, the choice between different judgments. The first rule in decision-making is that one does not make a decision unless there is disagreement.

The Effective Executive, *p. 148*

Questions

How do I develop alternatives for decisions that must be made? Do I suffer from undue influence from those in my organization who stand to gain or lose from my decisions? Do I stimulate the imagination of parties to a decision?

_____

_____

_____

_____

_____

_____

> ### First Who . . . Then What
>
> "Good-to-great management teams consist of people who debate vigorously in search of the best answers, yet who unify behind decisions, regardless of parochial interests."
>
> Jim Collins, *Good to Great: Why Some Companies Make the Leap . . . and Others Don't*, HarperCollins, 2001, p. 63

Actions

Develop a process for soliciting organized disagreement among your associates over decision alternatives. Make sure, by encouraging disagreement, that you are not lost in the fog when some of your decisions prove deficient or wrong.

The Decision

The effective decision-maker compares effort and risk of action to risk of inaction. There is no formula for the right decision here. But the guidelines are so clear that decision in the concrete case is rarely difficult. They are: Act if on balance the benefits greatly outweigh cost and risk. Act or do not act, but do not "hedge" or compromise.

The Effective Executive, *p. 157*

Question

Do I tend to hedge a decision if I know the decision is not going to be popular?

_____

_____

_____

_____

_____

_____

_____

_____

_____

_____

_____

Actions

Do not rush into a decision unless you are sure you under-stand what the decision is all about. But when the process has been followed and the decision is ready to be made, act or don't act, but do not hedge by, for example, asking for another study.

_____

_____

_____

_____

_____

_____

_____

_____

_____

_____

Conclusion

Effectiveness Must Be Learned

Best Hope to Make Society Productive

Effectiveness *must* be learned.

∽

Effectiveness reveals itself as crucial to a person's self-development; to organization development; and to the fulfillment and viability of modern society.

Self-development of the knowledge worker is central to the development of the organization, whether it be a business, a government agency, a research laboratory, a hospital, or a military service. It is the way toward performance of the organization. As executives work toward becoming effective, they raise the performance level of the whole organization. They raise the sights of people—their own as well as others'.

Executive effectiveness is our one best hope to make modern society productive economically and viable socially.

The Effective Executive, *pp. 166–174*

Questions

Am I more effective now than when I started this book? Which practices should I go back to and practice some more?

_____

_____

_____

_____

_____

_____

_____

One Bonus Practice of the Effective Executive

This one is so important that I will elevate it to a rule: *Listen first, speak last.*

Effective executives differ widely in their personalities, strengths, weaknesses, values, and beliefs. All they have in common is that they get the right things done. Some are born effective. But the demand is too great to be satisfied by extraordinary talent. Effectiveness is a discipline. And like every discipline, effectiveness *can* be learned and must be *learned.*

Peter F. Drucker, "What Makes an Effective Executive,"
Harvard Business Review, June 2004, p. 63

Where Do I Belong?

Successful careers are not planned. They develop when people are prepared for opportunities because they know their strengths, their methods of work, and their values. Knowing where one belongs can transform an ordinary person—hardworking and competent but otherwise mediocre—into an outstanding performer.

Peter F. Drucker, "Managing Oneself,"
Harvard Business Review, January 2005, p. 106

Level 5 Leadership

"Level 5 leaders display a workmanlike diligence—more plow horse than show horse."

Jim Collins, *Good to Great: Why Some Companies Make the Leap . . . and Others Don't,* HarperCollins, 2001, p. 39

Actions

You can learn to be an effective person and effectiveness must be learned. Train yourself in effectiveness. Assess your development in effectiveness periodically.

Authors' Note

In its aim, scope, and approach this book differs significantly from Peter Drucker's *The Effective Executive* (New York, Harper-Collins Publishers, 1966, 2002). But, *The Effective Excutive in Action* is based upon *The Effective Executive* and upon Peter Drucker's subsequent work on this subject. We did not hesitate to draw upon Drucker's recent work where appropriate to the objectives of this book.

The heaviest debt is owed to *The Effective Executive*. Most of the entries in this book are taken from passages of *The Effective Executive* as indicated by the references. In addition, many passages from two of Peter Drucker's recent articles in *The Harvard Business Review* ("Managing Oneself," January 2005, and "What Makes an Organization Effective," June 2004) were used to update and supplement original passages in *The Effective Executive*.

The reading on page 64 is adapted directly from the article "What Makes an Organization Effective" as are fourteen additional passages that are included as "sidebars" in this book.

The readings on pages 123–137 are adapted from the article "Managing Oneself" as are ten sidebars. Chapter Six is adapted partially from "What Makes an Effective Executive" and partially from material previously published in electronic form as well as from Chapters Six and Seven of *The Effective Executive*.

We would like also to acknowledge the use of twelve passages excerpted from an interview with Peter Drucker conducted by Rich Karlgaard, "Peter Drucker on Leadership," *Forbes.com*, November 19, 2004.

We also acknowledge the use of eleven passages from Jack Welch, *Winning* (HarperCollins Publishers, 2005); eleven passages from Jim Collins, *Good to Great* (HarperCollins Publishers, 2001); three passages from Jack Welch, *Jack: Straight from the Gut* (Warner Books, 2001); and two passages from Bob Buford, *Halftime* (Zondervan Publishing, 1994).

Finally, we wish to thank Knox Huston and Leah Spiro of HarperCollins for their help with this book. *The Effective Executive in Action* was Leah's idea. Knox Huston of HarperCollins was our editor for the book. They have our thanks.